The Emerging Pacific Community Concept: An American Perspective

A Staff Report on the
CSIS Pacific Basin
Congressional Study Group

Principal Chairmen
Senator Paul S. Trible Jr., Virginia (1983)
Senator S.I. Hayakawa, California (1982)

Robert L. Downen, Director
CSIS Pacific Basin Project

edited by
Bruce J. Dickson

September 1983

The Center for Strategic and International Studies
Georgetown University, Washington, D.C.

Price $5.00

909.09
E 53

Library of Congress Cataloging in Publication Data
Main entry under title:

The emerging Pacific community concept.

   1. Pacific Area cooperation.   2. Pacific Area—Strategic
aspects.   3. PacificArea—Foreign relations—United States.
4. United States—Foreign relations—Pacific Area.   5. CSIS
Pacific Basin Congressional Study Group.   I. Dickson, Bruce
J.   II. CSIS Pacific Basin Congressional Study Group.
DU29.E55   1983   909'.098230828   83-18862
ISBN 0-89206-048-4

85-8166

CONTENTS

Business

John R. Alison
Vice President for Customer Relations
Northrop Corporation

David Dean
Chairman of the Board
American Institute in Taiwan

Al Dendo
General Dynamics

W.H. Krome George
Chairman and Chief Executive Officer
Aluminum Company of America

Donald Gillespie
General Dynamics

John C. Marous
President-International
Westinghouse Electric Corporation

William F. McSweeney
President
Occidental International Corporation

William N. Morell, Jr.
Managing Director
USA-ROC Economic Council

Alfred O. Munk
Amoco

Ralph Pfeiffer, Jr.
Chairman of the Board and Chief
    Executive Officer
IBM World Trade Americas/Far East
    Corporation

Thomas Stern
Korea Economic Institute of America

The CSIS Congressional Study Group is addressed at its first session by Senator John Glenn, Study Group Cochairman. Looking on, from left to right: Robert L. Downen, Pacific Basin Project Director; Ray S. Cline, CSIS Senior Associate; and Senator S.I. Hayakawa, Study Group Chairman.

Also attending the November 16, 1981 meeting of the CSIS Congressional Study Group are (left to right): John Holdridge, Assistant Secretary of State for East Asia and Pacific Affairs; Senator Harry F. Byrd, Jr., and Congressman (now Senator) Paul S. Trible, Cochairmen of the Study Group.

Statement of the Chairman

All too often, American attention is focused on those areas of the world beset by tension and conflict. As a result, areas of significant American interest become areas of secondary importance. Yet U.S. interests are becoming increasingly enmeshed with the Pacific Ocean region, and this region and our interest there merit our concern.

The Georgetown University Center for Strategic and International Studies is to be commended for organizing a Congressional Study Group on the Pacific Basin Community concept. The purpose of this Study Group has been to increase the awareness of Americans— particularly members of Congress, scholars, and the business sector— regarding this little understood and relatively unexplored but highly important policy issue that is now under review throughout the region.

This CSIS staff report is an overview of the issues and ideas addressed by the Study Group. It is not a policy recommendation, nor a call to action; neither is it a unified perspective of the Study Group. Instead, it reflects the diversity of American perspectives on the Pacific Basin, based upon different professions and the differing opinions of individual members. The report, therefore, summarizes a wide range of American interests in the region for the benefit of scholarly analysis.

It has been my pleasure this past year to serve as chairman of this distinguished group and to participate in Study Group deliberations with my colleagues who served as Cochairmen: Senators John Glenn and Frank Murkowski; Congressmen Stephen Solarz and Joel Pritchard; former Senators S. I. Hayakawa (who served as Study Group Chairman during 1981–1982) and Harry F. Byrd, Jr.; and former Congressman Paul Findley. Their interest and involvement helped give the Study Group its vitality and sense of purpose.

I hope that this group, through its work, can help the United States recognize the great opportunities for cooperation that lie ahead in the Pacific Basin region and thus deal better with the challenges that lie before us in that region.

Paul Trible
United States Senator

Foreword

Over the past two decades, the Pacific Ocean has shrunk to a "basin," and it is still shrinking. Remarkable advances in communication and transportation, the evolution of multinational enterprises, and, more frequently, coinciding national interests have in effect drawn all the regional states into the same neighborhood. Like all good neighbors, many nations within and on the periphery of the Pacific Ocean have sought the means to coordinate their efforts more efficiently, to resolve their differences, and to ensure an improved standard of living. Despite vast cultural, political, geographical, and historical differences, most of the regional states agree that closer mutual cooperation is both necessary and desirable. This has led to the broad conceptualization of a "Pacific Community" structure.

In the fall of 1981, the Pacific Basin Project at Georgetown University's Center for Strategic and International Studies (CSIS)—with the participation of several interested members of the U.S. Congress—organized a multifaceted, informal task force in Washington to survey the Pacific Community proposal from an objective, scholarly perspective. The organizers sought out leading experts in the field of Asian-Pacific studies as well as those with specialized knowledge of particular relevant aspects of the Community issue. The new CSIS Congressional Study Group on the Emerging Pacific Community Concept was composed of scholars, policymakers, and business representatives interested in exploring the nature and the dimensions of regional community proposals, as well as the prospective role and pitfalls for the United States. That Study Group has met at periodic intervals over the last two years to focus on different topics at issue.

From the beginning, the participants agreed that there would be no attempt to encourage unanimity or to establish a consensus of opinion. Nor would the Study Group strive to produce any policy recommendations. The sole purpose of the group was to provide an academic forum for the free exchange of ideas and concerns among different professions concerning the Pacific Community concept in accordance with American perspectives.

Furthermore, all deliberations after the initial meeting were conducted off-the-record—that is, there would be no attribution of comments during the sessions to specific individuals. This understanding helped encourage an open and free exchange of thoughts. In this report, confidentiality has been preserved, with the participants' occupations cited only to give perspective. Names of individuals have been cited only in connection with comments made at the first public meeting in November 1981, or where permission was given.

Throughout the past two years, the CSIS Pacific Basin Project staff has been engaged in support activities for the Study Group, undertaking comprehensive research on Pacific Community proposals and developments; analysis of related political, economic, and strategic issues; individual country studies; and preparation of relevant background briefing material for Study Group members. In addition to the Study Group sessions, the Project also has sponsored a variety of seminars, conferences, lectures, and publications on regional issues.

Perhaps the greatest value of the Study Group deliberations, and of this report, has been the development of a broad-ranging approach to the Pacific Community proposal couched in a uniquely American perspective. Rather than approach the proposal specifically as a highly organized, institutional structure, Study Group members recognized that the Pacific Community concept encompassed a spectrum of alternatives ranging from informal to the very formal, from an exclusive membership to the broadly inclusive, and from government-sponsored to the completely nonofficial involvement of scholars and business representatives. Each alternative has its own special character and purpose, its own advantages and disadvantages. But the CSIS Study Group was interested primarily in the general concept of growing regional interaction rather than in defining or recommending a specific format.

The purpose of this report is simply to characterize the wide range of concerns, ideas, and observations brought forth by this eclectic grouping to provide interested observers in Washington and the Pacific region with some notion of professional thinking on this issue. This summary has been prepared by the CSIS staff according to memoranda of the several Study Group meetings and has been neither reviewed nor authorized by individual participants in those sessions. Because not all Study Group members participated in all meetings, and because opinions often were conflicting, it would be a mistake to associate any particular participant with any particular viewpoint or recommendation. Nor should any portion be construed as a CSIS institutional perspective. Instead, it is hoped that this report may in a small way contribute to an understanding of American perspectives on this complex proposal.

Robert L. Downen
Director
Pacific Basin Project
July 1983

Introduction

The concept of a Pacific Basin Community has been under consideration in various forms among Western Pacific scholars for several years. Virtually all those familiar with the idea have expressed some degree of interest, but no one has yet come up with a viable proposal that has received widespread support. And that is the essence of the problem: there is general agreement on the desirability of Pacific Basin regional cooperation but no one has been willing or able to propose an acceptable plan that could transform the Community idea into a tangible entity. In a sense, the Pacific Basin Community is an idea without a program, a goal without an agenda.

To bring into focus both the prospects and the problems involved in creating this Community, CSIS has sponsored a series of Congressional Study Group meetings to explore the concept, primarily in terms of economic cooperation. The Study Group convened its first meeting late in 1981, and over the next year and a half held other meetings on a periodic basis. These informal, off-the-record discussions have brought together members of Congress and leaders from the executive branch, academia, and the business community to engage in a free discussion of the prospective evolution and the practical nature of a Pacific Basin Community. Each participant brought to the Study Group an individual perspective derived from the participant's own background. Some had years of experience in the Asian-Pacific area and were well informed on the issues. Others had a more general background, of which the Pacific Basin was but one part. Still others had little or no experience in the area, but, like the others, felt that the Pacific Basin will acquire a more prominent role in America's future and wanted to become more familiar with the topic.

From its inception, the Study Group was viewed as an objective, scholarly task force designed to examine the pros and cons of American involvement in a Pacific Basin Community and, more broadly, the prospects of the development of such a community. Participants in this Study Group have discussed general U.S. economic and stra-

1

tegic interests in the Asian-Pacific region; the influence of the People's Republic of China (PRC), particularly the effect of the modernization program on regional development; the future role of Taiwan and Hong Kong in Asia; the increasing interdependence in the region, especially regarding trade and energy; proposals for regional summitry; and the essential role of the Association of Southeast Asian Nations (ASEAN) in any Pacific Basin organization.

The Congressional Study Group's seven discussions have revolved around three interlocking questions about the Pacific Basin Community: its desirability, its feasibility, and its specificity. There was no equivocation on the desirability of closer regional cooperation. Nearly all participants agreed that every vital actor in the area, and particularly the United States, can gain by the sort of cooperation that community consciousness could provide. But once the discussions turned to the feasibility of such a cooperative community and what functions it would serve, the Study Group voiced a myriad of opinions. What countries would be included in the regional concept? Should this be a governmental or unofficial grouping? Should it limit itself to economic and trade matters only, or should it also encompass security and strategic issues? Not surprisingly, there was little agreement on these questions, given their complexity and magnitude.

The absence of a single-minded conceptualization did not prevent— on the contrary, tended to stimulate—a productive and dynamic exchange of American perspectives on this generally neglected issue. This paper does not purport to represent a formal consensus of the CSIS Study Group, nor should it be confused as such. Rather, it is a summation of the various views and opinions expressed by individual Study Group participants in an unofficial setting.

1

Desirability: All Stand to Gain, but Who Gains What?

Nearly all the participants of the Congressional Study Groups generally concurred on the desirability of the Pacific Basin concept; furthermore, the Asian-Pacific nations themselves have expressed continuing interest in the idea through the years, though enthusiasm tends to ebb and flow. Such a community, in theory, would provide a context for lessening existing regional differences as well as a framework for more efficient economic development in what is currently the most dynamic economic region of the world. Cooperation among the countries in the area could be useful in removing or reducing trade barriers and investment restrictions. Reduction of trade barriers would be particularly important in the case of Japan, which has been amassing large trade surpluses with the various nations of the Pacific Basin, largely because of its exceedingly high tariff and nontarriff barriers, such as unreasonably high quality standards for imported goods.

A formalized grouping of nations could also internationalize bilateral disputes and conceivably reduce tensions. With the rapid development of the Asian Pacific nations has come a host of problems, including internal social pressures, trade imbalances, export competitiveness, and the scarcity of natural resources. Senator S. I. Hayakawa noted these conflicts in his introductory remarks to the Study Group. "But the important question," he concluded, "is whether such social and economic problems will be faced during the remainder of this century by a Pacific community of nations under leaderships that share common objectives and a sense of common interest, or whether the tensions they inevitably engender manage to dominate the interrelationships."

Asian-Pacific Regional Attitudes

The greatest benefit from cooperation, as perceived by the CSIS Study Group, would be increased trade opportunities, both within the region and as a result of a concerted approach to shrinking foreign markets. Intraregional trade constitutes more than 50 percent of the total trade for the Pacific countries. This interdependence has been steadily rising, due perhaps as much to perceived mutual benefits as to the lingering world recession. One aspect of this interdependence that could immediately benefit from regional cooperation is in the area of commodities. As former Ambassador Alexis Johnson pointed out during the opening session,

> At some point, any study of Pacific Community relations, especially one of a possible future organization, has to come to grips with the question of commodities: commodity prices, commodity trade, and commodity supports. One thing we have to remember about the ASEAN countries is that the pace of industrialization is very uneven. A number of these countries still depend on natural resources and agricultural exports as the main vehicle for economic development.

Some Study Group participants felt that a Pacific Basin Community could rationalize commodity trade and fend off future conflict, not only among the ASEAN nations themselves but also between them and the nations to which they sell their commodities. The United States and Japan rely upon the Pacific nations for much of their raw materials and natural resources used in the manufacturing process.

A related issue is the energy interdependence of the Pacific Basin. An entire Congressional Study Group session was devoted to this topic. It was pointed out during the formal presentation of Dr. Sevinc Carlson that the region is looking to diversify its energy sources. Japan has been trying to lessen its dependence on Middle East oil by increasing its purchases from Indonesia, Malaysia, and Brunei, and, to a lesser extent, China. During the recent oil glut, however, Japan was hoping to withdraw from some of its Indonesian contracts and take advantage of the bargain prices offered by Middle East producers. As one Study Group academician noted, when it comes to economic interest versus security of supply, Japan's choice is obvious. But one U.S. businessman disagreed, speculating that Japan would give a little on price if they could be assured a steady supply of petroleum. A third opinion, offered by another scholar, was that price is a "50–50" deal with the Japanese. It is diversification of supply, not security of supply, that is the crucial factor.

The Pacific Basin countries are also seeking to lessen their dependence on oil by switching to other forms of energy. Coal and natural gas are obvious examples, but perhaps of greater importance to the Pacific Basin Community is the development of alternative energy sources. The Philippines, for example, are leading in the development of geothermal energy. Manila already has one geothermal project in process and more plans for future development. New Zealand also has a plant and is giving technical aid to Indonesia, while Japan is also interested in assisting in Indonesia's geothermal development. Japan will then use in other countries the technology and experience gained there. In addition, Japan helps finance shale oil and tar sands development in various Pacific Basin countries. This sort of regional cooperation in new fields of endeavor is precisely what adherents of the Pacific Basin Community concept hope to achieve.

As was typical of many Study Group sessions, much of the discussion of ASEAN energy interdependence centered on China. This was indicative of the professional orientation of many of the participants, but also of the immense influence China potentially has over regional developments. China has begun to exploit its energy resources actively, including the granting of leases for drilling in the Bohai Gulf, Yellow Sea, South China Sea, and the Gulf of Tonkin and the agreement with the Occidental Petroleum Corporation for coal excavation in Shanxi Province. But the bulk of China's energy development will invariably go toward fueling its own modernization program, with very little left over for export.

Not many years ago, it had been predicted that China would be able to finance its modernization largely by the foreign exchange it would earn from the export of its offshore oil. Such projections have been sharply scaled down. China has not been able to increase its production of oil from onshore wells substantially, nor has it been able to proceed very far with the costly conversion of its industries from oil to coal-burning plants. Although one Study Group participant speculated that if China were unable to become an oil exporter there would eventually be a Pacific region oil shortage, other participants saw little danger of this occurring. The Asian-Pacific countries, they maintained, are not relying upon large reserves of Chinese oil to solve their energy problems. If anything, they are interested in Chinese oil for the sake of diversifying their supplies. China does export small amounts of its oil and coal, but mostly for the sake of maintaining political relations with its trading partners in the area.

The region has some serious problems that will become acute by the end of this century. One U.S. government official expressed the hope that the emergence of a Pacific Basin Community would enable Asia to deal more effectively with the long-term problems of food, population growth, energy, and urbanization. For example, a study

5

done by the Carter administration, using straight-line projections, showed that every major city in the world will double its population by the year 2000.* There are nearly a half-billion people in the West Pacific, plus more than a billion Chinese, a growth that shows little sign of abating. The problem of feeding, clothing, and housing this enormous population in such a concentrated area is truly a regional problem, and the desirability of cooperation on these issues is readily apparent.

American Interests in the Pacific Basin Community

There was little doubt within the group that the Pacific Basin is increasingly vital to U.S. economic and strategic interests. Total U.S. trade with the Asian-Pacific nations has surpassed trade with our Western European partners for several years and continues to rise. Although the current economic recession has prevented the value of trade from increasing, trade with the Pacific Basin countries as a proportion of total U.S. trade has risen steadily, climbing from 23.9 percent in 1978 to 27.5 percent in 1982. Senator Paul Trible expressed this view during the introductory meeting. "Most Americans," he said, "and especially those who live along the Eastern seaboard, tend to look forward Europe. Our ties historically have been with that region of the world. But in my judgment, the future lies in the Pacific. America as a Pacific nation must play an active role in the affairs of that region. . . ."

One of the main purposes of the Congressional Study Group has been to focus the attention of policymakers on Pacific Basin cooperation. Rapid economic growth combined with the relative political stability in the region is unmatched by any other area. Dr. Ray S. Cline pointed to the need to take advantage of some of these favorable developments. He expressed his hope that the Study Group would allow its participants "to get a hold of an understanding of the developing patterns that will affect the balance of power, the political evolution, and the economic evolution of that region before we are confronted with some grievous crises."

Several participants expressed concern that the United States had not yet in the early 1980s formulated a coherent and comprehensive Asian policy. Some believed that, by encouraging the establishment of a Pacific Basin Community, the United States can prove its desire to be an active participant in regional affairs and its willingness to

---

The Global 2000 Report to the President: Entering the Twenty First Century (Washington, D.C.: GPO, 1980).

U.S. Trade With the Pacific Basin Community
(U.S. $ millions)

	1978	1979	1980	1981	1982
Japan					
U.S. Exports	12,885	17,581	20,790	21,823	20,966
U.S. Imports	24,467	26,258	30,714	37,655	37,744
China					
U.S. Exports	822	1,724	3,755	3,603	2,912
U.S. Imports	325	594	1,057	1,895	2,284
Taiwan					
U.S. Exports	2,342	3,272	4,337	4,305	4,367
U.S. Imports	5,174	5,908	6,854	8,072	8,893
Hong Kong					
U.S. Exports	1,625	2,083	2,686	2,635	2,453
U.S. Imports	3,476	3,998	4,739	5,389	5,539
South Korea					
U.S. Exports	3,160	4,190	4,685	5,116	5,529
U.S. Imports	3,746	4,047	4,147	5,227	5,637
Australia					
U.S. Exports	2,912	3,617	4,093	5,242	4,535
U.S. Imports	1,659	2,164	2,509	2,464	2,287
New Zealand					
U.S. Exports	405	530	595	922	897
U.S. Imports	527	708	702	715	775
Indonesia					
U.S. Exports	751	982	1,545	1,302	2,025
U.S. Imports	3,627	3,622	5,217	6,022	4,224
Malaysia					
U.S. Exports	728	932	1,337	1,537	1,736
U.S. Imports	1,519	2,146	2,577	2,185	1,885
Philippines					
U.S. Exports	1,041	1,570	1,999	1,787	1,854
U.S. Imports	1,207	1,490	1,730	1,974	1,806
Singapore					
U.S. Exports	1,462	2,330	3,033	3,003	3,214
U.S. Imports	1,068	1,467	1,921	2,114	2,195
Thailand					
U.S. Exports	629	961	1,263	1,170	915
U.S. Imports	439	600	816	946	884
ASEAN Sub-Total					
U.S. Exports	4,611	6,775	9,177	8,799	9,744
U.S. Imports	7,860	9,325	12,261	13,241	10,994
Grand Total					
U.S. Exports	28,762	39,772	50,118	52,445	51,403
U.S. Imports	47,234	53,002	62,983	74,658	74,153

Source: U.S. Department of Commerce

work for the mutual benefit of its constituent nations. The Pacific Basin countries are mindful of the relatively low priorities generally assigned to the area by the United States and are sometimes dubious of U.S. motives there. Therefore, some Study Group discussants asserted, U.S. interests can be best served by clearly stating U.S. objectives and working on behalf of regional cooperation—but in a subtle manner, taking care not to "plunge in and take over."

There also needs to be a clearer understanding of the role of the United States can play in Asia through private enterprise. One business representative pointed out that the activities of private industry on an individual level, rather than at the often insensitive governmental level, should be encouraged. In addition, he suggested the American public needs to become better educated about the history and culture of Asia. Americans must learn how to deal effectively with the people of Asia in a mutually beneficial way.

U.S. interests in the Pacific Basin Community are not only economic but also include the region's political stability. In this respect, not merely regional interests are involved. In the larger view, U.S. global security interests are also served by fostering an atmosphere of cooperation and collegiality in the Pacific area, thereby denying the Soviet Union or other aggressive nations an opportunity to interfere in regional affairs. Although most Congressional Study Group members were careful not to overstress the political and strategic implications of a Pacific Basin Community organization, they suggested that such considerations cannot be totally separated from any discussion of economic, energy, maritime issues, even if they are not explicity at issue.

In addition to the positive economic and strategic benefits to the United States, some Study Group participants argued that there is a strong negative inducement for American cooperation: The United States is in danger of being shut out of regional affairs because of its own negligence and events beyond its control if it does not adopt a more active, tangible policy soon. The potential leadership succession crisis in the Philippines, U.S.-Sino conflicts over U.S. cooperation with Taiwan, and the intermingling of trade and security matters with Japan all threaten to come to a head in the next two or three years. The United States could, as some suggested, find itself in an unfortunate, isolated position. The danger that lies ahead is not a continuation of the status quo, but a situation that one participant described as "status quo-minus."

The Response So Far

Beyond a general spirit of agreement concerning the desirability of a Pacific Basin Community, the substantive response among the governments in the region has been mixed and for the most part muted. Several functional task forces are now at work, but few proposals have been put forth so far and no comprehensive regional decisions reached.* The reasons for this are several, varying from nation to nation and depending on their respective roles in the region.

The U.S. response to the concept has been the most typical: official interest and monitoring of developments but no established policy. The U.S. government has been listening with interest to private opinions about the idea, but has not as yet actively pursued the idea. There are two explanations for this response. First, the United States simply has not focused much attention on the Pacific Basin as a region and therefore does not have a single coherent policy to use as a framework for either considering or promoting the concept. Assistant Secretary of State John Holdridge told one early session of U.S. attempts to solidify its relationships with Asian countries, especially the ASEAN group but also Australia and New Zealand, which he maintained should be included in the discussion "because they are politically, economically, and strategically adjuncts of the whole system we are trying to see develop." But U.S. policy has not really congealed here, and several Study Group members believe this must change quickly if the United States hopes to retain its influence and benefits in the area.

Second, and of equal importance, is the prevalent perception that the United States cannot take the lead on this issue. This is, and should be, an "Asian-Pacific proposal." The United States can voice its support and quietly encourage other countries to consider the idea, but Washington should avoid the appearance of trying to dominate the area. The same holds true, some participants suggested, for Japan and perhaps even Australia. The developing ASEAN countries are highly sensitive about large power domination and will remain skeptical about any proposal that they perceive has hegemonic overtones. Recollections of U.S. dominance and Japanese imperialism have by no means faded. The absence of U.S. leadership in this area therefore may reflect a rare example of sensitivity to regional concerns. "I don't think that this [concept] can be an American imposition on that area," said Senator John Glenn at the first session of the CSIS Study Group.

---

*A conference held in Bangkok in 1982, which followed the Pacific Community Seminar held in Canberra the previous year, implemented four task forces that are now researching four possible areas of regional cooperation: (1) investment and technology transfer, (2) trade in manufactured goods, (3) trade in agricultural products, and (4) trade in mineral commodities. These task forces have been established in Japan, South Korea, Thailand, and Australia, respectively, and will report their findings at the next regional conference to be held November 21–23, 1983 in Bali, Indonesia.

"It is something we want to encourage, something like ASEAN. . . . Maybe it will be self-generating so that it is not something that is looked at as a Pacific NATO that would require taking military overtones along with it. That would scare people . . . particularly the ASEAN countries."

The ASEAN nations themselves have been occasionally supportive but generally noncommittal in their response to the Pacific Basin concept. "The main obstacle," Assistant Secretary Holdridge argued, "is the reluctance of ASEAN to get involved in a broad organization which may not be attentive to its primary interests." Some representatives of ASEAN do not feel their organization has solidified yet. The success of ASEAN so far has been due to the closely shared interests of its members. They have little intention of becoming prematurely entangled in a larger undefined, multilateral organization. They are not, however, blind to the idea, only content to wait for a concrete proposal that they could consider. They must be convinced that there is more to be gained by joining than by going it alone.

Japan, however, has played a crucial role in initiating the idea of a Pacific Basin Community. In January 1980, former Prime Minister Masayoshi Ohira, an early proponent of the Pacific Basin, made the first official proposal. His administration encouraged a scholarly dialogue that has continued to this day in Japan, but his proposal was not well received by other countries. Japan has recognized the need for regional cooperation but also the importance of maintaining a low profile. Like the United States, a too vigorous approach by the Japanese could be self-defeating.

Ironically, Japan's motivation for pursuing regional cooperation is due in part to its successful economic development. Its aggressive export trade policy has run up a sizeable trade surplus, but has also antagonized its trading partners who trace many of their economic and unemployment problems to the invasion of Japanese imports into their domestic markets. Japan now exercises a measure of self-restraint in its foreign trade, and cooperation with its trading partners has become essential for Japan's maintaining its free access to foreign markets.

Equally important to Japan's interest in the Pacific Basin were the "oil shocks" of the 1970s, which exposed Japan's dependency on foreign sources of energy. It therefore sought more reliable energy sources from the Pacific Basic countries, particularly Indonesia and Malaysia.

During the summer of 1982, South Korean President Chun Doo Hwan made one of the few formal proposals for initiating a Pacific Basin Community. He suggested a series of summit conferences attended by the heads of state of countries interested in regional cooperation. The invitation was open to all countries with Pacific borders, regardless of their economic system. The open door aspect of President Chun's proposal set it apart from most others and also was at variance with the opinions of most of the participants of the Congressional Study Group. The general consensus in the Study Group has been that a Pacific Basin organization would best include only the nations with free market economies, at least initially. One member of Congress asserted further that a U.S. president should not attend any summit conference "unless something good is going to come out of it by prearrangement." But one scholar proposed that there would be an educational value to developing a regular set of high-level meetings. "It is educational in an economic sense rather than being political or security related," he said. The economic importance of Asia still needs to be brought home to the American public, American business, and even to Congress.

China does not have a declared policy in the Pacific Basin Community. Several years ago, the Chinese were promoting the idea of regional cooperation, but for anti-Soviet objectives. Since then, there has been little public discussion of the topic, either in the press or by PRC officials. One academician told the Study Group of the apathetic response of PRC Foreign Ministry officials to the idea. Chinese officials seem doubtful that the PRC could have much of a role because of its drastically different economic system and have difficulty seeing how the PRC could fit into such an organization.

2

Feasibility: Making the Process Work

Although there was no major disagreement among Study Group members over the desirability of the Pacific Basin Community, at least in theory, the question of feasibility brought forth a wide variety of opinions. Some held that, in time, the necessity for institutionalized regional cooperation would prevail, overcoming the inertia that has developed in the many years this idea has been under discussion. Others were less sanguine, feeling that some of the problems cannot be considered lightly. Still others wondered if there was even an informal Community to speak of, regardless of how the word is defined. Ultimately most participants in the discussions agreed that if Pacific governments were to perceive possible advantages on specific functional issues—such as sea-lane security or energy interdependence—by pursuing multilateral over strictly bilateral relations, the impetus toward an officially sanctioned, formal Pacific Basin Community would be enhanced.

The concept of a Community need not, of course, imply a formal organization of Byzantine complexity. There are various gradations to the Pacific Basin Community, ranging from casual discussion groups, to groups that meet on a regularly scheduled basis, to a highly structured organization. Less formal groups, such as the task forces that grew out of the 1982 Bangkok meeting, have their role to play at present. They bring together concerned parties of different professional backgrounds to keep interest alive in the concept.

There is little history of formal cooperation in the Pacific Region. Much has been made of developing an ASEAN variant of the European Economic Community, but the comparison does not hold. The nations of Europe have closer historical and cultural ties. Moreover, Europe had the legacy of two world wars and the threat of Soviet encroachment to make cooperation more a question of necessity. The Pacific Basin has little of this. For the most part, these countries have quite distinct historical, religious, and ethnic heritages. There is not at present a universally perceived military threat to the region, nor can any one country threaten the others single-handedly. But the memory of Japan's imperialistic adventures in the area remains vivid. Japan obviously would have to play an important role in any Pacific Basin Community, but the other countries are wary of Japanese economic domination of the area and some have become alarmed by indications of renewed militarism.

But from the perspective of economic and trade issues in particular, these nations have very much in common today. Implicit in the Study Group discussions was the recognition that the lack of enthusiasm for the Pacific Basin Community stems in part from unwillingness to accept concessions necessary for cooperation. The whole region is experiencing dramatic economic growth and industrial development almost simultaneously. Countries that rely on export-led growth invariably compete for many of the same markets. Their governments stand or fall on economic trends. As the current worldwide recession shows, in times of trouble most countries tend to go it alone. The Pacific Basin countries may feel they have *too much* in common to make formal cooperation feasible.

The only practical example of formal regional cooperation to date is ASEAN. Its success has been due to the narrow goals it has set for itself and the scope of its activities, taking care to steer clear of the taint of superpower collaboration and overt strategic considerations. For the Pacific Basin Community concept to gather momentum, the ASEAN countries must be convinced that their specific interests will not become submerged in the larger process. Several Study Group participants noted that it is important for the United States not to try to transform ASEAN into a political organization beyond its limited objectives. The self-image that ASEAN has created for itself is part of the problem. As one Study Group participant put it, ASEAN cannot agree within itself where threats to its welfare originate. Each ASEAN country individually determines where its own interests lie. It is not always easy to decide how their interests can be complementary nor how the various socio-economic systems and cultures can be meshed for the common good. Yet the ASEAN experiment has worked remarkably well.

Although there is little other formal cooperation in the Pacific Basin, all of the countries still seem to be open to the idea of at least informal but regular consultations. What is needed is a timely, attractive proposal to bring the concept into practical focus. One widely shared opinion held by Study Group members was that the most advantageous way to start would be with small, informal functional groups to show the viability of larger cooperative endeavors. If several of these functional groups proved effective, they conceivably could then be grouped together into a larger, more formal entity. Some Study Group participants believe that it is better to begin in this incremental way rather than by building a large superstructure, then attempting to find ways to fill in the shell. Any ambitious proposal not based on proven results would probably have little chance of success.

There were several suggestions offered during Study Group discussions as to how to establish a foundation for engendering support for the Pacific Basin Community. One academician, noting that the natural basis for a Pacific Community is weak in comparison with the European Community model, suggested six ways to overcome this obstacle:

1) U.S.-Japanese cooperation in providing gentle great-power leadership on behalf of the process;
2) More emphasis on subregional development along the lines of ASEAN;
3) Greater attention to the functional aspects of providing the transfer of technology from the developed to the developing countries;
4) Continued strategic and military stability with deterrence of the Soviet threat as a unifying objective. In this view, the benefits of broad regional economic cooperation would perhaps dissuade the North Koreans and Vietnamese from engaging in destabilizing activities;
5) Promotion of grassroots exchanges to compensate for distance and cultural problems;
6) Deemphasis of China's role in a potential Pacific Basin economic community, because China's modernization program is leading it in a very different direction from that of the free market developing nations in the region.

One businessman listed several basic fears and apprehensions that still exist in the area. The continuing tensions on the Korean peninsula, Vietnam's domination of Indochina, the dispute between China and the United States over arm sales to Taiwan, and Soviet interference in the region all hinder cooperation among the Pacific Basin nations. One of the distinguishing characteristics of the region is that these examples of instability actually militate against increased cooperation. In other areas of the world, nations faced with similar problems have tended to band together to seek a solution to bilateral conflicts before they exceeded their boundaries and became regional and even international

14

crises. Not so in the Pacific Basin, and that is what makes any discussion of the issues so delicate.

Although much discussion centered on China's developmental problems and its distinctive features, which set it apart in the area, a China scholar suggested that there may be certain contributions China can offer to its regional neighbors as a group. This participant mentioned the obvious examples—the benefits of trade, economic, and military cooperation—but also elements of the Chinese experience that could be relevant throughout Asia. These would include urban management, population control, and medical care. China itself often emphasizes reciprocity as the cornerstone of its relations with foreign countries, this scholar noted, and it is important for the Pacific Basin countries to realize what they have to gain from China.

Taiwan also has made its contributions to the region. At one session, a participant noted that Taiwan has sent agricultural teams to various Pacific Basin countries to assist in directing land reform programs. Taiwan provides the largest container shipping facilities in Asia and is rapidly becoming a major financial center, attracting a share of the capital leaving Hong Kong. Its tourism industry is also growing because of its relatively stable prices. Finally, although it has few natural resources of its own, it has developed a flourishing export trade in textiles, electronic products, and plywood. These factors in combination with Taiwan's high rate of personal savings and good debt-service ratio indicate that Taiwan has much to offer as a model for economic development, several participants agreed.

Finally, an extention of trust and confidence from one Pacific Basin country to the next is needed. There are too few examples from the past to learn from or build upon. If a Pacific Basin Community is to be forged, it will have to be flexible enough to meet the needs of all its diverse members and to accommodate future growth, but it will also require the strength necessary to survive the difficulties that are sure to arise. This was the third question taken up by the Congressional Study Group: What are the specific characteristics of the much discussed, but seldom defined, Pacific Basin Community proposal?

3

Specificity: The Shape of Things to Come

The issue of specificity provoked the most discussion during the Study Group sessions. Each suggestion about the composition and role of the Pacific Community had supporters and detractors, and there were still others who felt certain ideas had merit but were not timely. The most troublesome of all was the question of membership. The argument, simply stated, in this: If you cannot agree upon what the Pacific Basin Community is or what it should hope to achieve, how do you determine who should be allowed to join?

The Membership Dilemma

The predominant view among Study Group members was that the Communist countries should be excluded, at least initially, and that membership in a Pacific economic community should be limited mainly to Pacific area nations with free market economies: the ASEAN countries, Hong Kong, Taiwan, South Korea, New Zealand, Australia, Japan, Canada, and the United States. This proposal is essentially for reasons of simplicity—to avoid the problems associated with major differences between centrally planned and free market economies. Conceivably, the Pacific Basin Community could include any nation with a Pacific border or any that interacts regularly with the region, stretching the defination of "community" almost to the point of making it meaning-less. Still, the notion of including Latin America was mentioned and discussed by the Study Group.

The most frequently discussed membership problem was the PRC-Taiwan political dichotomy. Some Study Group participants felt that the membership problem in general, especially with regard to China, does not need to be resolved prior to the establishment of a Pacific

Basin organization. But certain future problems in this area seem so inevitable that they need to be considered at once.

Most participants of the Study Group believe that PRC should not be a member for the present. But the Study Group also concluded that the China market and China's exports will be primary economic factors in the Pacific Basin for years to come. One participant suggested that an important benefit to be gained by regional cooperation is the opportunity for joint proposals to China, because China's development needs are too large for any single country to provide for adequately. Under present circumstances, it is difficult to envision formal contacts and exchanges between China and a Pacific Basin Community in which Taiwan is an official partner. Neither China nor Taiwan would be wholly comfortable with such an arrangement. One China scholar conjectured, after watching Beijing's reaction to U.S. and Dutch exchanges with Taiwan in the last few years, that there is little reason to be optimistic about Taiwan's involvement. It would have to be done in a quiet way that would be "successful in promoting a fruitful interchange without resulting in an international incident."

It may not be necessary to include the PRC, but antagonizing it would serve no purpose. China could resort to a spoiler role if it felt its interests were threatened. First, it probably would protest loud and long against any institutionalized Pacific Basin Community that had Taiwan as a formal member. Second, a Pacific Basin Community that encircles China but has no role for it and that shuts it out of regional trade would put Beijing on the defensive. Third, China seems to prefer bilateral relationships to multilateral organizations. A recent article in *Beijing Review* outlined China's role in Asia; nowhere did it mention regional cooperation on trade or economic matters.* This being the case, other countries may feel they have more to gain through bilateral relations with China than by being a part of a Pacific Community.

Both China and Taiwan may be willing to deal with each other in the workings of a Pacific Community if there is no explicit *official* connection. This supplants the question of membership with the less onerous question of participation. This may be a distinct possibility in the future, as evidenced by the sending of the director-general of the Civil Aviation Administration of China to Seoul in connection with the hijacking of a Chinese passenger plane to South Korea. Perhaps this is the way to get around the membership dilemma: focus attention on participation in informal functional groups, not on membership in an official organization.

---

*Pei Monong, "China's Future Position in Asia," *Beijing Review*, April 18, 1983, pp. 15–19.

17

Although there may be ways of sidestepping the question of membership, there is no way of solving it. One academician was critical of the South Korean proposal for a formal summit conference because "it raises the membership issue in the historical context in a way that it cannot be answered." For a Pacific Basin Community to succeed, it has to be structured in such a way that the membership issue does not become a barrier to the cooperative effort. Otherwise, there cannot be cooperation between countries that do not maintain official diplomatic relations.

The question of Soviet membership was not as controversial. It was pointed out that the Soviet Union has not shown much interest in being a part of any Asian community structure. One participant suggested that Moscow would only be interested in the Pacific Basin to the extent of reaping certain advantages. By limiting the scope of the Community's actions, the Soviet Union could preempt a potential threat. Still another academician argued that Moscow is in fact not attempting to maintain the status quo in the Far East but is making stronger attempts, primarily with its military support of Vietnam, to change the course of events for its own benefit. In this view, the Soviets intend to alter or control the economic direction of the Pacific Basin by continuing to be militarily oriented and trying to gain political influence in the area. The general sense of the Study Group seemed to be that the way to prevent Soviet interference in the Pacific Basin would be to give the Community an anti-Soviet stance and consequently exclude it from membership.

The Future Status of Hong Kong

Also discussed was the future status of a natural member of the community, Hong Kong. China has stated clearly that it intends to restore its sovereignity over Hong Kong once Britain's lease expires in 1997. It is not clear, however, how China intends to administer Hong Kong after that date. The benefits provided by Hong Kong are numerous and crucial to China's well-being. Between 30 and 40 percent of the PRC's foreign currency is earned in Hong Kong. It has invested $2 billion in recent years, runs hundreds of companies, operates 13 banks, and has substantial land holdings. Hong Kong is its number one port for both imports and exports. Hong Kong has also become a frequently used channel for countries who wish to trade with China but do not have diplomatic relations. When sovereignity over Hong Kong is recovered by China, however, this last advantage will be lost. Hong Kong will lose its safe distance from Beijing, which provided the ease and anonymity of indirect trade.

China has much to gain by allowing Hong Kong to retain its present status. But anxiety within the colony's commercial sector is growing owing to uncertainty over China's intentions. Already, the flight of capital from the colony has begun, and the Hong Kong dollar has sunk to historic lows. China has said very little about how it intends to administer Hong Kong beyond vague references to provisions for special administrative zones in the newly adopted constitution. The PRC has declared it will not take action to invoke its authority over Hong Kong until 1997, and, although some 14 years remain before the lease expires, the more time that elapses without progress in the Sino-British negotiations, the more confidence in the future of Hong Kong is jeopardized. At stake is the continued prosperity of the colony and of much of the Pacific region. Because Hong Kong's economy is based on the service sector, with only secondary attention to the manufacturing industries, Hong Kong lacks the resiliency to withstand a prolonged crisis of business confidence.

In a formal presentation to the Study Group, one China scholar suggested three prerequisites for maintaining business confidence in the colony. First, the maintenance of the Hong Kong monetary system is essential. Free currency is a fundamental part of Hong Kong's success. If China shows any inclination to interfere with this exchange system, confidence would erode drastically. Second, the maintenance of the Hong Kong legal system and its related institutions is important. Third, some form of disinterested administration is necessary to ensure current ease and simplicity of operation. Hong Kong is the last bastion of laissez-faire capitalism, unencumbered by the restraints of public policy. This is Hong Kong's strongest asset and at the same time the area where it is least compatible with China's economic system.

The Study Group claimed no reliable insight into the future resolution of the status of Hong Kong. All hoped for a successful outcome, but members had varying degrees of confidence in the ability of China's leaders to come to a suitable arrangement. One academician maintained that China could afford to live without the benefits derived from Hong Kong, implying that Beijing therefore would be willing to do so. A U.S. administration official echoed this, stressing that "the Communists just do not understand the capitalist system." The Chinese appear to be concerned above all with sovereignty and have said they will not sacrifice sovereignty for the sake of economic considerations.

Much of the uncertainty over Hong Kong's future stems from the delicate balance of the Chinese position. On the one hand, China must tread lightly so as not to disrupt Hong Kong's economy brazenly. If its prosperity is destroyed as a result of the PRC's administration, Taiwan will have even stronger reason to resist Beijing's reunification proposals. Moreover, as a result, international opinion could swing toward sympathy for Taipei's resistance. On the other hand , China feels it must take a firm stand as a matter of national pride. Hong Kong was the first colony ceded to a foreign power during the decline of the Qing dynasty, and its current colonial status is a constant reminder of the humiliation dealt to imperial China. Peking feels it must prove to the world, and especially to Taiwan, that it means what it says about regaining territory that rightfully belongs to it, regardless of the cost. The contradiction between these two positions is so extreme that in the end, one might conclude, the fate of Hong Kong will likely stand at one extreme or the other; there seems little likelihood of reaching an accomodation in the middle.

Security Interests in the Pacific Basin

Beyond the question of who would be a part of the Pacific Basin Community and what the role of each would be, the Congressional Study Group discussed the nature of the organization and how the Community would be initiated. The consensus was that the only workable solution is for the Community to start in a small way, accumulate experience and confidence, then expand. Some suggested it would be best to begin with an organization set up to solve specific mutual problems rather than promote mutual benefit in general. Several suggestions were given as a functional basis for cooperation such as sea-lane security, energy interdependence, and the setting of fair commodity exchange rates. Of these, the issue of sea-lane security met with broadest interest.

In his opening remarks to the Study Group, Congressman Paul Findley said, "The safety of the sea-lanes and coastal areas are a growing concern of nations great and small. The question of the safety of the sea, with or without military connotations, is certainly a logical part of the investigation of the Pacific Basin Community." Other participants were in general agreement on the importance of the issue. The Pacific Basin countries may be reluctant to discuss regional security issues, but they will discuss preserving their vital commercial links to each other. The security of sea-lanes could provide one organizing concept for a Pacific Basin Community. It is a modest beginning, based on a basic issue of immediate importance that would be of equal benefit to all the nations of the Pacific Basin.

For much the same reasons that the Congressional Study Group agreed on the merits of starting in a small way, they also agreed that the United States and Japan should take pains to avoid taking a leading role. Both must support the idea—but from well behind the front lines. If either appears overbearing it will arouse suspicions and may inhibit acceptance of the idea. The United States has neglected to pay close attention to the Pacific Basin for so long that it must move slowly but decisively to prove the sincerity of its interest in the area to avoid giving the appearance of opportunism.

The Study Group was divided on whether or not the Pacific Basin Community should serve an overt security function. Some felt that discussion about sea-lane security naturally involves overtones of military cooperation. One academician felt one of the keys to the success of the Community was the fundamental assumption of an anti-Soviet stance. Another urged more caution: "Let security be discussed in the corridors and when and if it becomes a common enough interest, a security aspect will naturally evolve into organized discussions." In his view, the danger lies in overstating the potential of a Pacific Basin Community: if there is not a common interest in security then there probably will not be much functional interest.

Many participants said that the Community should stay absolutely free of military and strategic objectives. All talk of strategic considerations, regardless of their desirability, is apt to backfire. The key to the whole Pacific Basin concept is the active participation of ASEAN— an idea pointed out many times in many contexts. The pursuit of strategic goals would carry with it a firm anti-Soviet slant, which is anathema to ASEAN's policy of nonalignment. Moreover, this might suggest U.S. domination of the organization, because no other country has a comparable military capability. But the United States must not appear as the leader of a Pacific Basin Community, either by advocating its creation too ardently or attempting to define its goals. If the United States makes too much of the strategic implications of regional cooperation, the other Pacific Basin countries may doubt the sincerity of the U.S. desire for more basic forms of cooperation, especially economic.

Facilitating Exchanges

What, then, is the role of the Pacific Basin Community—to make the region stronger and more cohesive or to make it more competitive in the world market? Implicit throughout the Congressional Study Group sessions has been the idea of "facilitation." The basic purpose of a Pacific Basin Community is to facilitate intraregional exchanges and to provide channels for communication, technology transfer, sea-lane security, and other commonly shared interests.

The facilitation of technology transfer among the Pacific Basin countries will be the most tangible result of cooperation. The region is interested in development based upon projects rather than products—in other words, a preference for software over hardware. The suggestion that regional development should be based on the comparative advantage of each country has not been broadly welcomed. Developing countries see it as a ploy by the developed countries to maintain the unequal levels of industrialization in the region. The developing countries prefer to obtain the technology for themselves to exploit and develop their own resources rather than rely upon the continued export of their raw materials to fuel economic growth.

The suggestion was made that the United States should not be overly concerned about the economic development of the Pacific Basin. A businessman was asked during one of the Study Group sessions whether he felt United States was doing itself a disservice by exporting the technology that may allow these countries to compete with the United States in the future. He replied that the United States does not have a monopoly on technology and that if the United States is not willing to share its technology, the developing countries (and he was speaking of China in particular) will find supplies elsewhere. "We must reconcile ourselves to the fact that we no longer have an unthreatened technological lead, but are in a competitive global market." The danger to the United States lies not in the transfer of our technology, he suggested, but to the loss of its competitive edge. The United States must be prepared to assist in the development of the Pacific Basin and to meet the challenges therein, because the Pacific Basin will develop with or without U.S. participation.

The consensus of the Study Group was that regardless of its size, scope, or membership, movement should begin soon toward the establishment of a cooperative Pacific Basin Community. The concept has been favorably discussed for years but has not received much substantive response. An important reason for this, it was pointed out to the Study Group, is that no one as yet has pointed out an overriding advantage to membership in such a Community structure. For that matter, there have been very few definitive proposals of any kind. Until there is more practical discussion, the Pacific Basin Community is likely to remain primarily conceptual.

The real virtue of South Korean President Chun's proposal, some suggested, was that it was an attempt to interject some life into the idea. Most agreed that it was a poorly timed proposal but that at least it was a tangible idea and therefore warranted some attention. The fact that there have been few counterproposals begs the question of how badly the Pacific Basin countries are interested in the idea after all.

Conclusion

The purpose of the Congressional Study Group has been to highlight the importance of the Pacific Basin as the region of the world currently experiencing the most dynamic economic growth. Congress, the executive branch, academia, and the business sector have cooperated in drawing attention to the absence of a well-defined American policy toward the region. It is time for the United States to come to terms with its Pacific trading partners, acknowledge its interdependence, and end the prolonged U.S. neglect of the region.

The potential for a Pacific Basin Community structure and the desirability of the benefits it could provide are understood and generally supported throughout the region. A Community already exists, as evidenced by the high rates of intraregional trade. If cooperation among the Asian-Pacific countries has been irregular up to now, it is equally true that this informal manner has been partially responsible for the sustained high growth rates of those countries. The nations of the area agree on the desirability of cooperation because it has worked so well on an ad hoc basis in the past. But it is on the issue of more formal, institutionalized cooperation that the consensus begins to weaken. The present form of low-key cooperation has been so beneficial that the countries involved are reluctant to jeopardize a proven, successful arrangement.

Although there is inertia aplenty in the Pacific Basin, there are forces at work to bring about more structured forms of cooperation. These include the numerous informal discussion groups, the task forces established at the 1982 Bangkok meeting, as well as frequent conferences and seminars. Better developed ideas such as the South Korean proposal are useful for keeping the idea alive and for fine-tuning the characteristics of a formal organization. What is needed now are practical measures that will transform simple talk into action. Only when the discussion moves away from the peripheries and begins to address the specific framework for cooperation will a Community in a formal sense begin to take shape.

The ASEAN countries, to some degree, have resisted a wider framework for cooperation while their own group is still taking shape. Perhaps their view should be more closely considered. Rather than plunging ahead into some newly constructed organization built on the basis of broader regional cooperation, perhaps an interim solution would be to give already existing institutions a more substantive role to play. Until the countries of the Pacific Basin, particularly ASEAN, are convinced that there are greater benefits in institutionalized cooperation than in the status quo, there is little likelihood of forging new ground.

Beyond the question of how to cooperate is the question of who should cooperate. The CSIS Study Group discussed at length the problem of China, which looms so large as a potential market for regional trade and which also promises to affect the role and status of Taiwan and Hong Kong. Any discussion of the specific characteristics of a Pacific Basin Community invariably deals with the membership issue, especially as it relates to China and its unique position in the region and potential for influencing regional events.

There are a variety of functions a formal Community may undertake. A primary task is facilitating exchanges between the countries. Of greatest importance is the transfer of technology from the developed to the developing countries so that economic growth is based on projects, not products. Another possibility is the range of strategic interests. Some Study Group members felt that strategic considerations were a natural outgrowth of regional cooperation, especially in the area of sea-lane security; others felt that such talk would unnecessarily alarm some countries and conceivably reduce their support.

The Study Group did not arrive at a formal consensus. Its purpose was not to recommend any particular policy but instead to generate enthusiasm and familiarity with the concept. Underlying each of the discussion sessions was the tacit acceptance of the need for greater American attentiveness to regional affairs. The United States runs the risk of being locked out if it does not replace its policy of studied neglect with one or more active participation. A greater share of America's trade goes towards the Asian-Pacific countries than towards Europe, but that economic truth has not yet carried over into the political field. As the trend of the last few years has shown, the future of the United States will become increasingly intermingled with that region of the world. But it will reap the full benefits of regional cooperation only when it develops a coherent policy that properly promotes American interests in the Pacific Basin Community.

APPENDIX

The Abacus Economy in a Computer World: China's Emerging Role in Pacific Basin Trade

by John C. Marous
President—International, Westinghouse Electric Corporation
(delivered February 2, 1982)

Many of you may remember the John Keats poem that describes the explorer Cortez's legendary moment of discovery:

> . . . when with eagle eyes
> He stared at the Pacific—and all his men
> Looked at each other with a wild surmise
> Silent, upon a peak in Darien.

In the past decade, or so, a lot of us—in business, in government, in the academic world—have been discovering—or rediscovering—the Pacific. But unlike Cortez and his men, our discovery hasn't been at all silent. In fact, we've been pretty vocal in sharing our "wild surmises"—and I think that's all to the good. A topic as vast and as vital as the Pacific Basin *deserves* a lot of talking about. So, when Ray Cline asked me if I'd participate in this study group, I frankly was delighted.

Westinghouse has had a long and very extensive involvement in the Pacific Basin. That involvment goes back roughly 100 years . . . to the days of George Westinghouse who set up an Australasian subsidiary as part of our corporation's first global effort. More recently, Westinghouse has been involved in technology transfers throughout the Pacific Basin. We've had a relationship with our largest licensee—Mitsubishi Electric in Japan—for almost 60 years. And our operations—in the form of subsidiaries, exports or licensing—extend to almost every country in the region.

But beyond those parochial interests, I really believe that the Pacific Basin is going to be assuming a much greater importance in the world economy—and in world affairs—than ever before. We've already seen a phenomenal amount of growth there in just the past few years.

The eight countries of the so-called "Pacific Growth Rim"—Hong Kong, Indonesia, South Korea, Malaysia, the Philippines, Singapore, Taiwan, and Thailand—have already become the fastest-growing subregion of the world, with the real growth rates reaching, and even exceeding, the 10 percent mark in recent years. What's more, according to major studies by Wharton Econometrics and Chase Econometrics, those eight countries are forecast to continue growing at an average, sustained rate of close to 10 percent through the Eighties and will more than double their real output of goods and services by 1990.

Add to that an even more remarkable success story in Japan that's growing more awesome as Japan commits itself to the "information era," as well as a continuing resource boom in Australia, and I think you can get a feel for the kind of future I'm talking about.

Already, those of us in business are witnessing the phenomenal competitive strength of these Pacific countries. Their companies have staked out major markets in every corner of the world. They're aggressive, they're highly mobile, and they're unusually resoureful in overcoming the many complexities of international trade. Japanese computers, South Korean steel and Taiwanese calculators are already pushing their way into world markets, and a vast array of new products is close behind. That's not even to mention those countries' capabilities in handling major project business, the monumental scope of their trading companies, or the magnitude of their human resources. So, I don't think it's any exaggeration to say that, at least in economic terms, the Pacific is fast outstripping the Atlantic.

Of all the countries in the region that I've visited and done business with, I think that China probably has the most uncertain role in the economic future of the Pacific Basin. At the same time, China holds the greatest store of human and natural resources in that corner of the world, and its potential impact on trade and economic growth in the Pacific Basin could be very substantial.

Today, I'd like to describe Westinghouse's own experience in China. I'd also like to offer a few observations based on our experience that, I hope, will shed some light on what other, technically more advanced countries can expect from China's "abacus economy."

Our involvement with China has been growing for roughly four decades. As far back as the 1940s, 100 Chinese engineers came to the United States and were trained by our company in the technologies of power generation, transmission, and distribution. Today, many of those same engineers hold senior positions with government ministries.

Some 30 years later, in the aftermath of President Nixon's China initiative, our company played a leading role in organizing the National Council for U.S.—China Trade and in helping to direct its activities. The Council's first chairman was our former Chairman of the Board Don Burnham.

In 1974, our involvement with the Council convinced us that a major corporation couldn't ignore China's enormous market potential. We decided that our only course would be to launch a persistent, low-key marketing effort despite the uncertainties and despite the improbabilities of any short-term gain.

One of the important lessons we learned as a result of our China involvement was that you don't *sell* to the Chinese, you *allow* them to buy. So, we set forth a three-part marketing plan: one, to demonstrate our corporate capabilities; two, to show the sincerity of our desire to do business with China over a long period of time; and three, to gain recognition as a cooperative—and communicative—business partner.

Our first step was to appoint a representative to act as a mediator between China and our company. That led to the exchange of countless delegations, and in 1976, it resulted in our first order, for the power generation equipment used on Boeing 707 jets. To accelerate our program, we proposed a technical symposium to the government in 1975, but received a response that was somewhere on the far side of lukewarm.

Finally, on January 1, 1979, our government established normal diplomatic relationships with China, seven years after the first negotiations were opened. Naturally, that greatly improved *our* corporate negotiating position.

Once again we proposed our technical seminar, this time to the China Council to promote international trade in Beijing. With that new proposal, our man in Washington suddenly became a shuttle diplomat. During three trips to Beijing extending over three months, he visited more than 20 ministries represented on the Council. During his visits, he had to present a summary of *each* subject we wanted to cover and explain to *each* minister why the symposium would benefit China. Our proposal was accepted early in 1979, and the symposium took place in Beijing that November.

The Beijing symposium lasted one week. It consisted of more than two dozen individual seminars and involved some 40 of our scientists and engineers. One measure of the symposium's success was its attendance: more than 400 Chinese came to hear what we had to offer and stayed for the entire week. Another measure of our success was the fact that the Chinese asked us to stage a modified version in Shanghai a week later—a request we were happy to grant.

But the *best* yardstick of our effort was a multimillion dollar contract for steam turbine technology transfer and related components, a contract we fully expect to be extended for many years to come. That China contract, by the way, chalked up a number of firsts for both Westinghouse and the United States in the China market. It was a first for the American power generation industry, a first for the U.S. Export-Import Bank, and a first for Westinghouse in the technology transfer area of our business.

Following on our success, we set up an office and stationed a country manager in Beijing. In addition, we continued our communications with the Chinese and reaffirmed long-standing relationships through our participation in a series of U.S. trade exhibitions.

Today, the number of our active negotiations has increased dramatically. We're negotiating technology transfer contracts for a number of our products and direct sales contracts for others. We're also a registered company with an office in Beijing and are promoting the unique concept of a joint Westinghouse-Chinese technology interchange center in the PRC. That center would house planning, orientation, training, and technical programs and could serve as a planning board for industrial development in the PRC.

In short, our long and often frustrating years of negotiation finally have paid off. In the process, we've learned that in doing business with the Chinese, you've got to have four attributes: you've got to be patient, persistent, fair, and consistent. Of course, it also helps to be able to hold your mao-tai.

◆ ◆ ◆

Obviously, our experience has made Westinghouse bullish on China. The Chinese economy is projected to grow by 4.5 percent next year and 6 percent a year thereafter. Trade with the United States has doubled in just three years, and the new openness to foreign technology should accelerate that pace.

Chinese planners are being more realistic about what can and can't be accomplished. The government is fiscally conservative and wants to pay as it goes whenever possible, in order to keep its debt burden at a manageable level. Free market methods are now looked on as suitable in certain situations. The Chinese are flexible and astute enough to abandon policies that don't work.

But while we at Westinghouse have a very positive outlook on China's economy, I think that all of us need to be mindful of the very real constraints on the development of China's vast economic resources. Above all, I think we in the technically more advanced countries need to recognize that we, as much as the Chinese, have the responsibility for finding an appropriate level of technology transfer to optimize China's economic growth. If we attempt to push China too far too fast, if we try to exceed her natural development constraints in the pursuit of some hoped-for "China bonanza," I'm afraid we'll be hurting ourselves as well as the Chinese. And that could, in turn, greatly hinder the development of the emerging Pacific Basin community.

In the time that remains, I'd like to make some observations about three factors I've seen that I think will play an important role in China's future growth: energy, management, and culture. I don't intend these observations to be encyclopaedic; whole books could and, in fact, have been written on each of those areas. I also recognize that there are other growth factors in China's economy—agricultural development, for example—where I have no expertise whatsoever. But these observations *are* based on my direct experience of doing business in China.

First, *energy*—since much of our efforts at Westinghouse have been directed toward the development of China's electrical energy potential. I think we have to recognize that while China's energy reserves are vast, those reserves are often very hard to get at.

Although estimates differ widely, China's coal reserves clearly rank among the largest in the world. Roughly three-quarters of those reserves, though, are concentrated in just six northern provinces. By the same token, China's oil reserves are also among the world's largest—but much of that petroleum production potential lies offshore: in the Bohai Gulf, the Yellow Sea, the East China Sea, the Taiwan Strait, the South China Sea, and the Gulf of Tonkin. And, until recently, China's offshore drilling capability was restricted to depths of under 130 feet.

According to a study soon to be released by the Association for Energy Study of the Chinese government, China will be giving high priority to the development of hydroelectric power. The study estimates that to achieve China's modernization goals, the Chinese will need to increase the proportion of electricity generated through hydropower from the current 19 percent level to 25 percent by the year 2000.

There's no question that China's hydropower potential is very large—in fact, probably the largest in the world. Some estimates rate China's hydropower potential at 680,000 MW—greater than the total generating capacity of the United States.

But the challenge, once again, is where that potential lies and the cost of developing it. Unfortunately, most of those untapped sources are situated in Tibet and in the mountainous provinces of the southwest—far away from the major industrial centers. That will pose a major challenge—not only in the enormous effort to construct dams in those hard-to-reach areas but also in developing the necessary transmission and distribution capability to get that electricity where it's needed.

How far does China have to go in developing its electrical potential? Well, currently in Chinese use only about 3 percent of the electricity consumed in the United States on a per capita basis. The Chinese per capita consumption today is roughly that of, say, Bolivia. In order to achieve its economic goals, China will have to at least quadruple its electrical usage by the year 2000. Even in China achieves that ambitious objective, their per capita consumption of electricity in the year 2000 will be only about the same as that of Chile today. To arrive at their goal, China will have to add almost as much generating capacity as now exists in the southern United States! Clearly, that's a major challenge for the Chinese—and a growth constraint that China's trading partners need to be aware of.

A second factor in China's economic development—and another major challenge—lies in industrial management. As many of you know, light industry has been given a great deal of emphasis by China's leaders in recent years. But I think that one of the major constraints on the development of that industry will be a lack of trained management—particularly at the middle management level.

The political disruption of the Chinese system of higher education during the 10 years of the Cultural Revolution has been a major roadblock to finding sufficient management resources. Nearly every university as well as many technical schools were completely shut down for that entire, 10 year period. What is more, it has only been in the past few years that university enrollment has returned to pre-Cultural Revolution levels. The net result has been that almost a generation of managerial talent has been lost. In fact, the Chinese Vice Minister Wang of the First Ministry of Machine Building frankly admitted to me that in his opinion the major constraint on China's development was the critical shortage of managers and technicians.

In particular, I think that China will have to concentrate very heavily on improving in two key areas—in productivity and quality management—if they want to gain the additional foreign exchange they'll need to begin to integrate themselves into today's global marketplace. Fortunately, productivity and quality are two areas that many of the countries in the Pacific Basin have developed to a very high degree, and I think they have an unprecedented opportunity today to share those skills with China.

My final observation concerns China's culture. Perhaps because China is such a vast country, many of us outside China—and I'll confess businessmen are perhaps most guilty of this—tend to look at China in terms of the numbers. And the sheer size and scope of those numbers often cause us to see what China could be—or what we'd like her to be—rather than what she is. And we tend to become impatient when the potential seems so far away from the reality. Some U.S. companies, unfortunately, tend to look at markets opportunistically rather than strategically. And when their China effort doesn't earn a quick return, they fold their tents and go home.

As I think I've tried to indicate, our approach at Westinghouse has been different. We've tried to recognize that the Chinese will only do business with those outsiders they really know. And it takes a pretty long time—in our case 40 years—to get to really be known and respected by the Chinese.

Naturally, as China's trade with the outside world increases that cultural lag will begin to diminish. In fact, that's already starting to happen. When one of those visiting engineers I mentioned earlier was having a final farewell dinner with my family, I asked him what there was about the United States that he found different from what he'd been led to expect.

He said to me: "I'm having trouble finding the capitalist." I asked him what he meant by that. He said, "Well, some years ago in China we used to be told about the American capitalist. He was depicted as the rich man who oppresses the workers. But from what I have seen, there is no capitalist. Everybody is rich, but no one is really oppressed. Everybody—the factory worker, the taxi driver, the office clerk—is a capitalist!"

Perhaps as our cultural interchange with China grows, more and more of those barriers will begin to break down. But until they do, outside companies will have to remain patient and persistent—as well as both fair and consistent in their dealings with the Chinese.

Above all, we have to recognize that China's culture and civilization has been evolving for thousands and thousands of years. Its language is the world's oldest continuously-used language, whose writing dates back 3500 years. That makes for a very powerful sense of history and a very powerful cultural inertia.

So, while the Chinese legitimately want and need Westernized technology, they don't necessarily want or need Western cultural values. Like many other highly traditional societies—the Islamic societies for example—their need for the technology of Western civilization is strongly counterbalanced by a need to preserve their own distinctive cultural values. They want progress—but Chinese progress, not American progress, or Japanese or Korean progress.

That won't be an easy thing for the Chinese to achieve, nor will it be easy for us to help them do it. But I'm convinced that the place to start is with a respect for the fundamental values of the Chinese culture. Nothing, in my opinion, could be more counterproductive to trade with China than to attempt to profiteer in the China market— to look for quick and handsome rewards from our investments in China.

With that thought in mind, I'd like to leave you with Chinese parable that I think those of us interested in the future of trade with China would do well to keep in mind. As the story goes, many years ago there was man from Ch'i who had a passion for gold. One day at the crack of dawn he went to the market straight to the gold dealers' stalls, where he snatched some gold and ran. Of course, the police quickly caught him. One of the policemen said to the man: "With so many people around, how did you expect to get away with it?"

"When I took it," the man said, "I saw only the gold, not the people."

I think we need to see in China not what glitters but what is.

Energy Interdependence in the Pacific Basin

by Sevinc Carlson
Director of International Energy and Southeast
Asian Studies, CSIS
(delivered April 28, 1982)

In order to have a balanced discussion of the energy interdependence in the Pacific Basin, one has to consider all forms of energy, that is, fossil fuels such as oil, natural gas, and coal, and alternative energy resources such as hydropower, geothermal, solar, nuclear, biomass, and others. The inclusion of all energy resources in such a discussion is necessary for three reasons.

First, although most Pacific Basin countries are dependent on imported oil, especially from the Middle East, they are trying very hard to switch from oil to either domestic or imported coal and other alternative energy sources.

Second, there are many Pacific Basin countries, such as the United States, Canada, and Australia, which import oil but export other forms of energy such as coal, natural gas, and nuclear energy.

Third, there are some Pacific Basin countries, such as Indonesia and Malaysia, which are net exporters of oil, but which also import oil from other sources for domestic consumption. These countries might become net importers of oil by the end of this decade unless they discover extensive additional oil reserves or develop alternative energy sources. Indonesia and Brunei are important liquefied natural gas (LNG) exporters, and Malaysia, Australia, Canada, and possibly Thailand, will in the future also become LNG exporters.

A few Pacific Basin countries, starting with those that are industrialized, will be used as examples for discussion purposes.

Oil Importing Industrialized Countries of the Pacific Basin

United States

The United States is a good example of a Pacific Basin country that both imports and exports energy.

The United States was the third ranking oil producer in the world in 1980 with 8.6 million barrels per day (b/d). If natural gas liquids production is included, the United States production for 1980 reached 10.2 million b/d of liquid fuels. However, the United States also had to import 6.9 million b/d of oil in 1980* as its domestic production was not sufficient to meet demand. Canada, Mexico, Indonesia, Malaysia, Brunei, Ecuador, and Peru were the Pacific Basin countries from which the United States imported oil.

The United States is also a large producer of natural gas. In 1980, it produced 20.4 trillion cubic feet per day of natural gas, but it also has to import natural gas from Canada and Mexico and LNG from Algeria.

On the other hand, the United States is the largest producer of coal in the world. In 1980, its coal production was 835.4 million tons. It is also an exporter of coal to some Pacific Basin countries like Japan and Canada. Japan hopes to increase greatly its coal imports from the United States if transportation and port problems can be solved. The United States will export LNG from Alaska to Japan.

Another important energy export of the United States to various Pacific Basin countries is in the form of nuclear power reactors and associated equipment and nuclear fuel—mainly to Japan, South Korea, and Taiwan.

Canada

Canada is also a Pacific Basin country that both exports and imports energy. Although it is an oil producer, it has to import oil for its eastern provinces while exporting some oil and natural gas to the United States. It will export LNG to Japan in the future. Canada exports nuclear reactors as well.

Japan

Japan produces very little domestic energy and has to import 87 percent of its energy needs. Oil contributes 68.2 percent of the imported energy and, in 1980, 73.2 percent was imported from the Middle East. Japan has been trying to diversify the sources of its oil imports, and in 1980, 19.8 percent of its oil imports originated in Southeast Asia, mainly from Indonesia, Malaysia, and Brunei, 3.6 percent came from the PRC, and 3.4 percent came from other sources, including Mexico.

Coal contributes 11.1 percent of the imported energy, and more than 60 percent of it is imported from Australia. The rest comes from the United States, the PRC, and other sources. Just as Japan is trying to diversify the sources of its oil imports, it is also trying to diversify its sources of coal imports and reduce its dependence on Australia because of labor problems in that country. Japan is also trying to

---

*U.S. oil imports have been decreasing steadily since 1980. For example, during the first 11 months of 1981, U.S. crude and refined products imports were only 6.1 million b/d.

34

increase its domestic coal production, which in 1979 provided only 2.9 percent of Japan's energy needs. Japan imported about 7 million tons of steam coal in 1980, but is projected to import between 130–140 million tons of coal in 1990 because of conversion from oil to coal in industrial and home use. Pacific Basin countries such as Australia, the United States, Canada, the USSR, and the PRC are expected to provide most of the coal needed by Japan by that date.

LNG contributes about 4.9 percent of Japan's imported energy, and its share in Japan's total energy imports and consumption is increasing. Japan currently imports LNG from Indonesia and Brunei. It will double its imports of LNG from Indonesia and will start importing LNG from Malaysia in 1983 and later from Australia, Canada, and Alaska.

Liquefied petroleum gas (LPG) contributes about 2.8 percent of Japan's imported energy. The bulk of it, about 80 percent, comes from the Middle East and close to 20 percent of it from Canada and Australia. Japan's LPG imports from Southeast Asia are currently negligible, but Japan plans to increase its LPG imports from that area.

Japan gives financial aid for—and both the Japanese government and many Japanese companies participate in—oil, coal, natural gas, shale oil, tar sands, and geothermal energy developments in various Pacific Basin countries.

Australia

Australia is a resource-rich country and both a current and future exporter of various energy resources to Pacific Basin countries.

Australia's current domestic oil production meets about 60–70 percent of its domestic needs, and a very ambitious onshore and offshore oil exploration and development program is being implemented to maintain the current production level of about 415 thousand b/d. As consumption is about 675 thousand b/d, the remainder is imported.

Australia is one of the three major exporters of both metallurgical and steam coal in the world and, in the Pacific Basin, Japan is one of its major importers. A pilot plant for coal liquefaction in cooperation with and funded by the Japanese government has already been approved. Australia is expected to make a significant contribution to the expanded coal demand in the 1990s.

In addition, Australia will export LNG to Japan and uranium to the Philippines in the future. It is also in the process of developing its oil shale resources. Consequently, Australia will play an important role in the future energy balance of the Pacific Basin.

New Zealand

New Zealand is another resource-rich Pacific Basin country that is a net oil importer. In 1981, 57 percent of its domestic energy needs were met with imported crude oil and LPG. Consequently, New Zealand's energy development program is oriented toward reducing this dependence to 35 percent by 1991 by developing its domestic energy resources such as hydropower, natural gas and natural gas liquids, and geothermal energy. Some oil has been found in the country and it still has undeveloped coal resources. New Zealand has signed an agreement with Mobil Oil to produce gasoline from natural gas.

New Zealand would like to import more oil from Indonesia and Malaysia to reduce its dependence on the Middle East.

New Zealand's contribution to the energy equation in the Pacific Basin takes the form of giving technical aid for the development of the geothermal resources of other Pacific Basin countries like Indonesia.

Oil Producing and Exporting Countries of the Pacific Basin

The USSR, the United States, Mexico, the PRC, and Indonesia are the major oil producing countries of the Pacific Basin, while Brunei, Canada, Australia, Ecuador, Peru, the Philippines, and New Zealand are the minor ones. (See Table.) Of these, the USSR, Indonesia, Mexico, the PRC, Canada, Malaysia, Brunei, Ecuador, and Peru are oil exporters. The others consume their production domestically.

Although the USSR is the largest oil producer in the world, most of its oil exports go to Eastern and Western Europe and it will not be discussed in this paper.

The United States is the second ranking oil producer in the Pacific Basin but does not currently export oil.

Mexico

Mexico's oil production steadily increased during the last few years. At the end of 1981, it was the third ranking oil producer in the Pacific Basin with 2.4 million b/d, after the USSR and the United States. Its oil production reached 2.5 million b/d in February 1982.

Mexico's oil exports also steadily increased during the last few years to about 1.1 million b/d in early 1982. Its plans were to increase oil exports to 1.5 million b/d by April 1982 and keep them at that level unless there was a change in oil production and export policy. However, some observers think that it will not be possible for Mexico to reach that export level. In the Pacific Basin, the United States is the

Estimated Oil Production of Major Oil Producers
(In million barrels per day)

Country	1960	1965	1967	1970	1971	1975	1979	1980	% of World Total 1980
USSR	2.9	4.8	5.8	7.1	7.5	9.7	11.9[3]	12.0	20.2
Saudi Arabia[1]	1.2	2.0	2.6	3.4	4.5	7.0	9.5	9.6	16.1
USA	7.0	7.8	8.8	9.5	9.7	8.4	8.5[4]	8.7	14.5
Iraq[1]	1.0	1.3	1.2	1.5	1.7	2.4	3.5	2.6	4.4
Western Europe	0.3	0.4	0.4	0.4	0.4	0.5	2.4	2.4	4.1
PRC	negl	0.2	0.2	0.4	0.5	1.4	2.1	2.2	3.6
Venezuela[1]	2.8	3.4	3.6	3.6	3.6	2.4	2.4	2.2	3.6
Nigeria[1]	negl	0.3	0.3	1.0	1.5	1.8	2.3	2.1	3.5
Mexico	0.3	0.4	0.4	0.4	0.4	0.7	1.6	2.0	3.3
Libya[1]	—	1.2	1.7	1.0	2.8	1.4	2.0	1.8	3.0
UAE[1,2]	—	—	—	0.7	1.0	1.8	1.8	1.7	2.9
Indonesia[1]	0.4	0.5	0.5	0.9	0.8	1.3	1.6	1.6	2.6
Canada	0.5	0.9	1.1	1.2	1.3	1.4	1.8	1.5	2.5
Kuwait[1]	1.6	2.1	2.3	2.7	2.9	1.9	2.3	1.4	2.3
Iran[1]	1.0	1.9	2.6	3.7	4.5	5.6	3.1	1.3	2.1
Algeria[1]	0.2	0.6	0.8	1.0	0.6	0.9	1.2	1.0	1.7
Neutral Zone[1]	0.1	0.4	0.4	0.5	0.5	0.5	0.6	0.5	0.9
Qatar[1]	0.2	0.2	0.3	0.4	0.4	0.4	0.5	0.5	0.8
Ecuador[1]	negl	negl	negl	negl	negl	0.2	0.2	0.2	0.4
Gabon[1]	negl	negl	negl	0.1	0.1	0.2	0.2	0.1	0.2
Others								4.3	7.3
World Total	19.5	28.4	33.0	39.5	44.7	49.9	59.5	59.7	100.0

Source: BP Statistical Review of the World Oil Industry, The Oil and Gas Journal

1. Members of OPEC.
2. United Arab Emirates.
3. Includes natural gas liquids.
4. Excludes natural gas liquids. If natural gas liquids are included, U.S. production for 1980 would be 10.2 million b/d.

major importer of Mexico's oil, followed by Japan, Canada, South Korea, and the Philippines. Mexico may be able to export larger quantities of oil to the Western Pacific Basin countries when its Pacific Ocean ports are completed.

People's Republic of China

The PRC is the fourth ranking oil producer in the Pacific Basin with a production of a little more than 2 million b/d. China, however, consumes domestically most of the oil it produces. Its oil exports were fewer than 300 thousand b/d in 1981. Although the PRC has a very promising onshore and offshore potential, a World Bank report predicted that it may become a net oil importer by 1990 because of declining oil production and increasing domestic demand.

The PRC opened the first round of bidding for the right to develop its offshore oil resources in February 1982. After the biddings are completed and contracts signed, offshore production is expected to start in the late 1980s. China already produces a small amount of offshore oil in the Bohai Gulf.

Indonesia

Indonesia is another large oil producer in the Pacific Basin and produced an average of 1.6 million b/d in 1981. It was the largest exporter with about 1.1-1.2 million b/d. Because of the recent glut and the relatively high prices of its oil, however, its oil exports have been falling.

In the Pacific Basin, Japan was Indonesia's main oil importer in 1980, receiving 54.5 percent of Indonesia's oil exports. The United States was the second ranking importer of Indonesia's oil. Oil imports from Indonesia were about 5 percent of the United States' oil imports. Australia was Indonesia's fourth ranking oil importer in 1980, with 2.2 percent of Indonesia's oil exports.

Thailand, the Philippines, and South Korea are among the other importers of Indonesia's oil. Recently, South Korea and Indonesia signed a joint venture agreement to explore for oil in Indonesia.

As already mentioned, Indonesia has become the largest LNG exporter in the world. All of Indonesia's current LNG exports of more than 8 million tons a year go to Japan, and these exports will reach at least 15 million metric tons beginning in 1983. South Korea is also interested in purchasing Indonesian LNG and plans have already been made to build the country's first LNG receiving terminal.

Indonesia's proved oil reserves have been estimated at 9.5 billion barrels. With a production rate of 1.6 million b/d (which has been greatly reduced because of the recent oil glut), the reserve to production ratio is 16/1. Indonesia wants to increase its oil production to 1.8 million b/d by the end of 1983, both to keep up with domestic demand that is increasing at 10–12 percent a year and to maintain the oil exports at their current level. According to one estimate, to be able to increase production to 1.8 million b/d at a 16/1 reserve to production ratio, Indonesia has to add an average of 0.9 billion barrels a year to its reserves for five years. Although exploration activity has greatly increased, some observers doubt that reserve additions of that magnitude may be feasible.

Indonesia is also making great efforts to develop its alternative energy sources such as natural gas, hydropower, coal, and geothermal to meet the domestic demand for energy. It has greatly reduced subsidies on oil products for domestic use to curtail the increasing consumption. If Indonesia does not discover sufficient additional oil reserves, develop its alternative energy sources, and reduce domestic consumption, it may become a net oil importer by 1990.

Brunei and Malaysia

Brunei and Malaysia are also oil producers and exporters on a small scale.

Brunei produced about 230 thousand b/d of oil in 1980, most of which was exported to Japan with some to the United States. Malaysia produced about 275 thousand b/d of oil in 1980, most of which was exported to Japan with some to the United States. Brunei is already an important exporter of LNG to Japan with about 5.2 million metric tons in 1981. Malaysia will start exporting 6 million metric tons of LNG to Japan for 20 years starting in 1983. In Malaysia, domestic energy consumption has been increasing by 9 percent a year, and the Malaysian government has embarked on an ambitious energy conservation and development program both to conserve its oil reserves and to reduce its dependence on oil for its domestic energy needs from 95 percent currently to 50 percent by 1995.

Ecuador and Peru

Ecuador and Peru are also minor producers and exporters of oil in the Pacific Basin.

All the other countries of the Pacific Basin are net oil importers. Some of them like the Philippines, Australia, and New Zealand produce some oil for domestic consumption. As already mentioned, most of these countries are making great efforts to develop their alternative energy sources. In this respect, some of them are better endowed than the others.

Because of the increasing energy interdependence in the Pacific Basin, the strategic importance of this area is self-evident. Also, because of the still considerable dependence of the Western Pacific Basin countries on Middle East oil, the strategic importance of the Malacca, Sunda, Lombok, and Makassar Straits is also self-evident.

39

Korea's Role in the Pacific Evolution

by Seung Hwan Kim
Director, Korea and Northeast Asia Project, CSIS
(delivered December 8, 1982)

In July of 1982 President Chun Doo Hwan called for the creation of a "Great Pacific Age" by promoting closer cooperation among the nations of the Pacific Basin region for peace and prosperity. He was the first head of state in the area to suggest the bringing together of national representatives for a Pacific Summit Conference to meet periodically, similar to the annual meeting of the industrialized countries of the West or the British Commonwealth of Nations.

By taking the lead in such a proposal, the South Korean government would act as a catalyst for the Pacific Basin Community and serve as an instrument for identifying problems. According to the official government position, President Chun's motive was to promote economic and technological cooperation, trade, and cultural exchange. It is safe to say that he included security considerations for the maintenance of stability on the Korean peninsula.

President Chun based his recommendation on five basic principles, more comprehensive than any previously set forth by Japan or other Pacific nations:

1. The institutionalization of summitry.
2. Mutual "door-opening" toward all nations of the region.
3. The respect for sovereignty and the maintenance of reciprocity and equality.
4. The development of potential and the promotion of deeper and many-sided cooperation and exchanges.
5. Deeper cooperation between advanced and developing nations.

First, the Korean concept is heavily dependent upon government leadership to push for a fast-paced evolution of the Pacific Basin Community, rather than upon the private sector—scholars, economists, and businessmen—for the development of international dialogue.

Second, the Korean proposal remains flexible about membership in the prospective Community, but it appears to encourage participation of all Pacific-rim countries including Latin American nations and, in particular, the Asian Communist nations, including the PRC, the Democratic People's Republic of Korea, and the USSR.

Third, the Korean format upholds the principle of equal leadership within the structure and rejects domination of leadership by the larger powers.

President Chun's summitry proposal carries significant pros and cons. The fundamental issue is whether or not to promote Pacific regional cooperation by depending upon the political decisions of top government leaders. This approach may be the easiest and quickest way to resolve fundamental differences and form the institutional mechanism, yet it may result in highly politicized meetings, which would not serve the original objectives. Governmental activity is likely to produce large power domination because of the differences in national strength and the degree of economic development of the Pacific nations. Although equal leadership in the Community is emphasized in the Korean proposal, the smaller nations fear diminished sovereignty status. The five ASEAN states, in particular, are worried that the prospective institution will overshadow their association of nations and weaken it.

The Patrick-Drysdale report, one of the most authoritative papers on the subject of the Pacific Community, suggests leadership of the United States and Japan and the full involvement of the other countries in the organizational structure.*

A further issue is whether or not to invite or encourage Communist countries to participate in the Community. Some believe participation by the Communist countries will indirectly help to maintain stability in the area. Yet others see practical difficulties arising between the free market economies and the centrally controlled and directed economies.

The Patrick-Drysdale report recommends that the initial participation should be restricted to five major developed economies: Japan, Australia, New Zealand, Canada, and the United States; and nine developing market economies: South Korea, Taiwan, Hong Kong, Papua New Guinea, and the five ASEAN states (Indonesia, Malaysia, Philippines, Singapore, and Thailand) in concert with certain small Pacific insular nations.

The fact is that there has never been any public announcement by the Communist leaders regarding their interest in multilateral economic cooperation among the Pacific-rim nations.

---

*In mid-1979, Hugh Patrick of Yale University and Peter Drysdale of the Australian National University provided a report at the request of John Glenn, then chairman of the Senate Committee on Foreign Relations. The report called for the formation of a new Pacific entity to be known as the Organization for Pacific Trade and Development (OPTAD). It is one of the most authoritative and detailed papers on the subject of the Pacific Community, although it did not carry any official endorsement.

Korea's Interest in the Pacific Basin Concept

When President Chun announced his summitry concept, he stressed the importance of the Pacific Basin. "I think the Pacific will emerge as the undisputed center stage of world affairs following the 1980s," he said. It is well known that the Pacific Basin is becoming the world's most dynamic economic region. At present, the collective economic strength of this region exceeds that of the North Atlantic. Roughly one-third of all world trade takes place within the Pacific. The level of economic interdependence in the Pacific is high, for most of the nations in the area depend upon regional markets for more than 50 percent of their exports. Its abundant natural resources and important minerals are much in demand worldwide. South Korea benefits greatly from this activity, having world trade, as of 1981, of well over U.S. $45 billion, and it hopes to obtain increased opportunities for expanding its trade. Already South Korea has substantial trade with the Pacific nations. Fifty-two percent of its exports and 60 percent of its imports flow to and from its neighbors. Seoul's objective is to have the most important market economy in the Pacific region, with an outward growth strategy emphasizing trade.

The most detrimental factor to this economic development is the uncertainty of the politico-strategic situation in the Asia-Pacific region. The Vietnamese attempts to control all of Indochina seriously concern ASEAN nations and China; tensions between Peking and Moscow continue; and the possibility of violence on the Korean peninsula is a constant threat in the decade ahead. South Korea hopes to expand contacts with the Asian Communist countries, including China and the Soviet Union, to promote stability and security on the peninsula.

The new institutional cooperation among the Pacific Basin nations could also help restrain unilateral decision making by major Asian powers, particularly the United States and Japan, on important economic as well as political matters and increase the role of Seoul in the decision-making process. One of Korea's major worries during the remainder of this century is the possibility of Japan's taking over America's role in Asia if the U.S. commitment gradually weakens.

South Korea, as a middle-ranking power, has a sense of isolation in the Pacific region. It has never joined ASEAN, nor has it become a member of the Organization for Economic Cooperation and Development (OECD), an international group formed by 24 states, including Japan, Australia, New Zealand, Canada, and the United States. So far South Korea has maintained a delicate strategic stance on the peninsula, but a closer relationship with Pacific Basin nations will considerably improve its economic and security situation.

Although President Chun's recommendation for Pacific summitry appears to some to be premature and ambiguous, it could help to ameliorate the excessive bilateralism that has long existed in the region. It could help, also, to counter the growing trend toward trade protectionism on the part of the developed countries, import-substitution strategies in the developing countries, and vertical trade structures.

These appear to be President Chun's reasons for taking the initiative at this time.

The Pacific Basin Invitation and American Interests

by Matthew M. Gardner, Jr.
Director of Asian Studies, School of Foreign
Service, Georgetown University
(delivered December 8, 1982)

The Pacific Summit Conference proposed by Korean President Chun, in combination with other Asian proposals concerning the future of the Pacific Basin, provide a framework for our examination of a unique situation that is emerging in the Asian region. I submit for your consideration that these proposals are more than rhetorically related, that they reflect a deep-seated concern about the directions of American policy toward Asia, that they collectively constitute an invitation to the United States, and that it is in the interest of the United States to listen and to provide a positive response.

Taken individually, one can easily dismiss proposals, and their support, as those of a Korean president seeking to legitimize himself domestically and internationally, of a caretaker Japanese prime minister, of a Taiwan and Singapore whose futures are inextricably bound to their international relationships, of an Indonesia asserting its primacy in ASEAN, and of an Australia wishing to be seen as in Asia but not of it. Taken collectively, these expressions and proposals concerning a Pacific Age begin to define a future that is couched in the timeless vocabulary of Asian international relations: of *panch shila*, Bandung, and hegemony; of century-old Pan-Asian principles carried forward through the prism of the Greater East Asia Co-prosperity Sphere. They emerge from societies where consensus is found among the governing elite before proposals are publicly aired, and in which businessmen and scholars frequently reflect and elaborate a ruling consensus.

These discussions, which have been increasingly broached during the past six months, and reiterated at the November Williamsburg XII conference in Tokyo, have more in common than their vocabulary: they emanate from societies that have the greatest stake in the security of the Pacific Basin, yet they speak to economic, and not military, matters; they emanate from societies that have serious confrontations on their horizons, yet they do not seek to exclude any society; and they emanate from societies that have close relations with the United States. In this context, President Chun's proposal differs from others in degree, rather than in kind, departing from an emerging regional consensus of what should happen only to the extent that he proposes how it should happen. Subsequent discussion has revolved around the appropriateness of means, not ends.

Underlying this emerging regional consensus is a concern about American foreign policy in general and American policy toward Asia in particular. There are three dimensions to this concern:

♦ The first is strategic—a concern that the United States is pursuing its confrontation with the Soviet Union with a single-mindedness detrimental to other interests and opportunities in Asia.

♦ The second is related—a concern that American involvement with the People's Republic of China and pressure on Japan to increase its level of armaments will at best recreate a destabilizing past, and at worst promote Sino-Japanese hegemony in Asia.

♦ The third is economic—a concern that the United States is inadvertently disengaging itself from Asia, evidenced through diminished business competitiveness, subscription shortfall to the Asian Development Bank, or, more important, America's current unwillingness to associate itself with the results of the Law of the Sea Conference.

These concerns underlie what I believe to be an invitation to the United States to refocus its attention and, to some extent, to reorder its priorities. The rationale for this invitation is not difficult to discover. Virtually all Asian states seek to retain American military and economic involvement in Asia. In the military dimension, the United States is seen as a strategic counterpoise to the Soviet Union. More important, in many cases, Asian states view the United States as a tactical counterpoise to the designs of their own neighbors. In the economic dimension, the United States is seen not only as an economic resource in its own right, but also as an economic counterpoise to Japan. Without an American economic presence, Japanese economic growth could readily create excessive dependency in foreign trade and investment. As a result, the United States is frequently invited to involve itself in Asian affairs for reasons formulated by others. It is invited into strategic competition with the Soviet Union, into intraregional conflicts, and into economic competition with Japan, not because it is necessarily good for the United States, but because it is the goal of the states of Asia that have their own interests at heart.

The Pacific Basin invitation, however, provides a radically different dimension. It is uncommon that states with differing cultures would move toward a consensus on the potential for the future. With the ASEAN exception, there is not a strong tradition within Asia for multilateral endeavors, which the Pacific Basin initiative provides.

There is also a discomforting lack of opportunities for developed and developing societies to collaborate in an endeavor of mutual interest. The United States and its American neighbors have, in effect, been invited to reengage with potentially all of the societies of Asia in framing a collaborative, not competitive, Pacific relationship that places economic concerns in a priority at least equal to military and strategic activity.

Should the invitation be accepted? I believe that it should, and that it is very much in the American interest to do so. There are a number of reasons for this judgment that I would like to enumerate:

One, America's policy toward Asia has been almost exclusively dominated by its concern for Soviet objectives and for the policies of societies seen as Soviet surrogates. The Pacific Basin concept enables the United States to simultaneously explore a parallel policy framework toward Asia, or with Asia toward the Pacific, which is not inconsistant with its global strategic concerns about the Soviet Union, but which does not seek to exclude the Soviet Union from positive participation in Asian affairs.

Two, U.S. Asian policy has been lacking an economic framework, which has become increasingly frustrating as the economic dynamism of the Pacific area has begun to impact directly on the American economy. The Pacific Basin concept addresses broad areas of common economic interest between the societies of Asia and the United States, and it provides the opportunity to engage the old and new states of the region for common purposes in an area in which common capacity has been demonstrated.

Three, the concept holds the prospect of providing alternatives to the existing confrontations in Asia that are particularly dangerous for Asian and world peace: between South and North Korea, between Taiwan and the PRC, and between Vietnam and ASEAN. These confrontations, and other historical disputes over territory in the region, are being given a new impetus with the establishment of territorial seas and economic zones that are creating new neighbors through new borders. Asia and the Pacific have the potential for becoming an increasingly dangerous place through the proliferation of conventional and nuclear weapons, where serious contradictions are emerging in the policies being pursued by many states in the region, including Japan, the PRC, both Koreas, Vietnam, and ASEAN. I stress this point because there are some very strong incentives for the PRC, North Korea, and Vietnam to seek to engage themselves in the Pacific Basin endeavor. The modernization policies of China provide their own rationale. North Korea and Vietnam must be provided the opportunity to join the real world of the Asian present and future. Their isolation is dangerous for their neighbors and encourages and their dependency on the Soviet Union.

Finally, there is the perception of inadvertant U.S. economic disengagement from Asia. I believe that the perception may describe a reality and that the United States is missing a vital opportunity in not associating itself with the conclusions of the Law of the Sea Conference. Although a global regime, many compromise were made by other nations to accommodate U.S. objectives, and many Asian states played significant roles in bringing the regime to fruition. The controversy over competitive bidding between Japan and the United States for offshore Chinese oil exploration tracts carries with it a significant undercurrent of this issue. The Pacific Basin invitation provides an opportunity for reengagement, and it is valuable for that reason.

To say that U.S. interest strongly recommend participation in this Asian initiative ultimately confronts the realism of President Chun's proposal. Having argued that a desirable opportunity has been presented is not identical with saying that the opportunity is feasible. How exactly will the leaders of societies who do not legally recognize each other, to put some relationships in their mildest context, sit down together at periodic, institutionalized conferences? Perhaps President Chun's concept of summitry is a bit premature if we are to take the concept of "summit" in its traditional context. Perhaps in the first instance it would be useful to affiliate governmental representatives, or private individuals so designated, to join with the businessmen and scholars who have begun the exploration. Perhaps delegations would initially represent the peoples of the Pacific Basin societies, rather than their governments. Representatives from the divided Asian societies might be able to attend initial meetings under these circumstances, unencumbered with sensitive implications of recognition.

It is, however, not necessary that we focus extensively on all of these technical issues. The Pacific Basin initiative is, after all, largely an Asian initiative, and it might be well to rely on the diplomatic imagination of our Asian neighbors to create the framework in which the forum might occur. There are numerous aspects of diplomacy in Asia that lend themselves to a concept as unclear and far-reaching as the Pacific Basin. A process that seeks consensus, which does not require a meticulous agenda, where voting is not mandatory, seems particularly well suited to what is admittedly an ambiguous venture.

This leads to my final point. I find the Pacific Basin concept particularly attractive because of my belief that the United States should approach Asia with a sense of collaboration. This collaboration should invite Asian defintions and not simply be an exclusive statement of American goals and principles. A policy context that brings the United

47

States into common effort with the societies of Asia would be most useful. As the Asian states begin to define their own place in the world, America had best understand it and prepare to deal with it now. In the decades ahead, that understanding may be necessary. Should the societies of Asia gain a position in the world that rivals that of the United States, it would be very much in the American national interest to be looked upon as collaborators in the Asian success, not as those who ignored or opposed it.

America's Stake in a Western Pacific Collective Security System

by Robert L. Downen
Director, Pacific Basin Project, CSIS
(January 1983)

When we survey the panorama of U.S. global commitments during the remainder of this century, we find our nation increasingly bound to the Western Pacific region by a broad range of interests. Indeed, the network of interdependence among all the nations located on either side of the Pacific Ocean is becoming better established and more complex with each passing year. These bonds of mutual reliance are rooted in similar social and economic goals shared by the Pacific nations and will require greater attention to unity of action and fresh ideas for multilateral cooperation in meeting the common challenges that lie ahead. Not the least among these objectives is preserving the stability and security upon which continued progress depends. For this reason, regional threats may well require a more cohesive and integrated response by all affected nations in the future.

New Soviet Threats to the Pacific

The Soviet military force structure in the Western Pacific has expanded steadily in recent years, and there is no end in sight to this growth. At present, more than 50 Soviet army divisions are stationed in the Far East, most of them along the Chinese border, but a conspicuous contingent of 10 thousand troops has been deployed in the Kurile Islands just north of Japan. Since the late 1970s, the Soviet Union's supersonic Backfire bombers have been positioned throughout its eastern regions, capable of making strikes against Japan, Korea, or the Philippines, then returning to their bases without refueling. These strategic bombers supplement some 2,000 other Soviet combat aircraft based in the area. Approximately 120 nuclear medium-range and inter-mediate-range ballistic missiles are targeted against Asian territory and have been dramatically reinforced by about 75 of the newest SS-20 multiple warheaad intermediate ballistic missiles.

Many of the most impressive advances in Soviet military strength and power projection have taken place in Moscow's Western Pacific naval fleet, however. There has been a 190 percent increase in Soviet naval surface combatants and a 30 percent increase in submarines in recent years—many of them equipped with nuclear cruise missiles.

49

Moscow's new aircraft carrier, the *Minsk,* now permanently stationed in Western Pacific waters, is due to be joined by another nearly twice its size by the end of this decade. And the Soviet acquisition of air and naval facilities in Vietnam since 1978 has broadened the USSR's maneuverability substantially in this region. This expansion of Soviet power in the Far East now overshadows previous U.S. military superiority in the area, particularly as other U.S. commitments in the Indian Ocean have necessitated occasional drawdowns in U.S. Pacific force levels.

All of these substantial gains in the Soviet Union's military strength in the Asian-Pacific region raise serious questions regarding Moscow's immediate and long-range regional objectives. Clearly, in the short term, Moscow hopes to utilize its new military muscle to intimidate China, South Korea, and Japan; to neutralize U.S. regional influence; and to exploit thereby whatever political and military opportunities might develop during the 1980s. From a more long-term perspective, the Soviet Union undoubtedly hopes to position its forces to gain control eventually of the Western Pacific sea-lanes—so vital to strategic mobility, commercial trade, and oil shipments from the Persian Gulf in time of regional or worldwide crisis. To date, it has achieved rather remarkable success in moving toward these objectives.

In face of this massive buildup of the Soviet military presence in the Far East, and in view of its own commitments and priorities on an expanding scale internationally, the United States has sought a "quick fix" to counterbalance the Soviet threat while U.S. forces are being reconstituted. This has taken the form, on the one hand, of looking to China as a potential strategic partner, providing its military force structure can be modernized, and, on the other, of attempting to induce Japan to take on major new defense responsibilities in the Northwest Pacific. Both attempts are short-sighted, inadequate, and fundamentally unsuited to the purpose, however. Neither China nor Japan, at this time, can be counted upon as a wholly dependable strategic ally against Soviet adventurism, nor is reliance on either viewed as an acceptable solution by our other Pacific friends. China has no intrinsic military strength equal to the task at present nor will it have within the foreseeable future, nor does its new series of probes toward reconciliation with Moscow inspire confidence in its reliability. Japan, still restrained by a pacifist constitution and skeptical public opinion, will be years in rebuilding its military force capability any-where near the point of securing a 1,000-mile buffer zone around its islands. Furthermore, the prospect of massive Japanese rearmament, or of major infusions of U.S. military weapons and technology to China, incites fear and dread among most of our other Asian allies.

Importance of Regional Security Cooperation

A more practical and acceptable alternative does exist. An integrated network of closer security cooperation among all the non-Communist Western Pacific nations deserves priority consideration. At present, the 10 capitalist nations of the West Pacific—Japan, South Korea, Taiwan, the Philippines, Thailand, Malaysia, Indonesia, Singapore, Australia, and New Zealand—all share similar concerns about the Soviet threat and other regional security matters. Yet, security cooperation has been handled primarily on a piecemeal basis to date, generally through bilateral arrangements and individual treaties with the United States. What is needed is the gradual, efficient integration of those various security arrangements into a single coherent system of collective security cooperation.

What might begin simply as a flexible system of regular region-wide consultations among the 10 nations and the United States could gradually develop into more tangible combined methods of threat deterrence and conflict resolution. To be sure, there are several areas of potential cooperation involving matters of mutual concern to the 10 nations: for example, joint protection of sea-lane security; protection of critical mineral resources; and common policy approaches to such regional threats as Vietnamese aggression in Southeast Asia, expanding Soviet naval and troop deployments, Korean peninsular instability, and the uncertainties of Sino-Soviet relations. Member states also could seek a regional consensus on the legitimate scope and objectives of Japan's revitalized military role.

Specific methods of policy cooperation are more complex and will be examined below. But the important point is that we have to begin now to think in terms of a regional "security community" system, led but not dominated by the United States, to counter threats to Western Pacific stability effectively.

Talk of a forthcoming "Pacific Century" and of increasingly interdependent community ties among the nations in this fastest growing region of the world has become commonplace. The concept of a loosely structured "Pacific Basin Economic Community," modeled to some extent after the successful ASEAN experiment, has been fostered in recent years by regional leaders such as Masayoshi Ohira, Zenko Suzuki, Chun Doo Hwan, and Malcom Fraser and is discussed and analyzed from every angle by scholars and businessmen at countless seminars and conferences. The notion clearly is picking up steam as the nations of the Western Pacific collectively experience the benefits of a more interdependent transition to full industralization.

But in all the talk about the Pacific Community, its advocates have avoided the sensitive aspect of regional security cooperation with utmost care. As the trendiness of the Pacific Community concept gradually has caught on, the prospect of collective defense efforts has been treated as a taboo subject—too coarse a topic for genteel scholars or cautious politicians.

There have been certain reasons for this—the failure of SEATO being too fresh a memory for some, and the more distant memory of Japanese regional militarism too painful for others. But the reasons for devoting renewed attention now to security matters seem all the more urgent in view of region-wide concerns about protection of vital sea-lanes, Soviet power projection, instability on the Korean peninsula, and aggression in Southeast Asia. Indeed, the dramatic growth of Soviet air and naval power in the Western Pacific and open Soviet support for continuing aggression by Vietnam against its neighbors already have done much to forge common threat perceptions among the non-Communist nations of the Pacific rimland.

The Communist regime in China heretofore has played no small part in encouraging this consensus about the dangers of Soviet expansion. Even the normally passive ASEAN nations, committed as they are to a pacifist outlook are becoming visibly agitated and are devoting more attention to ad hoc security measures within their group.

Offsetting a Strategic Imbalance

In fact, the idea of collective Pacific Basin deterrence efforts makes good sense, both strategically and tactically. It is inherently more effective than simply relying on one or two nations in the area—Japan or China for example—to fill gaps in the current regional security imbalance between U.S. and Soviet forces. Secretary of Defense Caspar Weinberger recently toured Southeast Asia and the South Pacific to reassure Washington's friends that the United States is not about to weaken its own commitment to the area despite global policy strategies that place higher U.S. priority on defending interests in Western Europe and the Middle East. But the simple fact is that the United States, despite dedicated and increasing defense efforts (budgeted now at 6 percent of our GNP), cannot effectively guarantee the security of the Western Pacific region in case of coinciding conflicts in Europe or the Persian Gulf area. The Soviet Union, Secretary Weinberger took pains to note, now possesses the capacity to fight a two-front war simultaneously in the East and West.

This shortcoming is causing mounting concern among most of the non-Soviet bloc countries of the Far East—concern that is scarcely mitigated by prospects of Japanese rearmament or simply by Chinese Communist rhetoric directed against "Soviet hegemonism." Nor are neighboring nations necessarily reassured by the type of ad hoc security innovation the United States supports in Kampuchea, that relies on a quasi-alliance between the Communist forces of Pol Pot and two figures of questionable authority that failed earlier to control events in their country successfully. Collective regional security, on the other hand, promises not only to strengthen physically the means of deterrence, but to inspire security confidence and give U.S. forces greater flexibility in meeting crises elsewhere.

In view of this situation, it seems all the more remarkable that most public figures and private observers seem reluctant to speculate on the more logical alternative of collective Pacific Community security cooperation. The non-Communist nations of the Western Pacific share not only a happy coincidence of free market economies, but also common security interests based largely on the contiguous sea lines of communication that support those economies. The logical extension of their mutual interest in expanding commercial and technical cooperation is joint protection of the means for doing so.

There is no doubt that the rimland Pacific nations together possess the logistics, the strength, and the willpower capable of deterring Soviet adventurism. Taken together, the 10 "capitalist" nations of the Western Pacific cover 4,447,253 square miles of territory lying astride the most important sea-lanes and straits of passage. They boast a combined GNP in excess of U.S. $1.8 trillion (against U.S. $1.3 trillion for the Soviet Union). The combined number of their armed forces far exceeds that of Soviet manpower stationed in Asia and the Pacific. When the air and naval forces of the United States in the Western Pacific are grouped with those of Japan and South Korea alone, they approach total Soviet naval tonnage and number of combat aircraft. The potential efforts of these three nations then, in combination with somewhat greater logistical support by other non-Communist Pacific nations, suggest an impressive deterrent to further Soviet advances in the Far East. The fortunate geographical dispersion of the nations along the major oil shipment routes between the Indian Ocean and Northeast Asia reflects an important geostrategic asset in their common favor.

Methods for Approaching the Concept

Of course, there are major obstacles to even preliminary discussion of regional security cooperation. The diverse cultural, military, and political traditions of the nations create natural barriers to defense cooperation. In addition, the varying degrees of concern among these nations over comparative Soviet and Chinese threats and differences in perspective on issues such as Japanese rearmament and how to deal most effectively with Hanoi separate the policy views of their governments. But these differences need not obstruct common steps toward effective, efficient deterrence of destabilizing trends in the area.

Initially, collective Pacific security cooperation need not necessarily entail a regional defense treaty, or even military initiatives, for that matter. There are a number of cooperative security methods that can be exercised, short of a formally institutionalized or treaty-based alliance. In its most essential form, this West Pacific security network should consist of regular joint consultations, initially among mid-level policymakers and academicians, aimed at formulating ideas for the integration of "stability enhancing" measures. These might include coordination of regional planning for develoment assistance and technology exchanges, more efficient distribution of critical mineral resources, policing of sea-lanes, and joint intelligence gathering and sharing operations. Certainly one major goal of regional cooperation would be security foresight: to identify potential common threats and joint means for deterring them. This might well result in agreement among high-level officials on combined diplomatic action for confronting Soviet expansionism in the area, for example. Given the critical importance of access to the major sea-lanes of communication spanning the Pacific arc from Japan to the Indian Ocean, the regional partners may next want to coordinate better their force deployments and basing patterns to guarantee certain sea control and sea denial capabilities in times of crisis.

At an even more advanced level, the 10 non-Communist nations could eventually facilitate their means for collective containment and resolution of regional conflicts by establishing training exchange programs for military personnel, multinational force exercises, and perhaps even by creating joint staffing arrangements to coordinate better regional military responses. It is worthwhile noting that much of this is already underway on a small scale, bilateral basis in the area, even among the ASEAN nations, and does not preclude maintaining a fairly flexible partnership that respects individual policy rights.

Logically, the United States, as de facto defense coordinator and capitalist model for the 10 Pacific nations, should take the lead in addressing this sensitive subject. Washington currently maintains bilateral security arrangements with the majority of these 10 nations, and most if not all of the group still views the U.S. defense force as the linchpin of Western Pacific security—facts that give the United

54

States a unique opportunity and responsibility for promoting the security community concept in a low-key, tentative manner.

Moreover, it seems practical that the security concept should be allowed to evolve simultaneously, but separately, from the formation of a Pacific Basin Economic Community structure. In the first place, the concept of an economic community structure is better developed and more politically and intellectually palatable at this stage; it should not be unduly encumbered by adjunct moves in other directions. Second, a different set of actors—both governmental and nongovernmental—may be involved in the two conceptual forums, at least initially. Finally, the relative success or failure of more advanced steps toward economic cooperation may indicate the likelihood of success in striving for some type of security arrangement.

Still, movement toward a loosely defined collective security arrangement should begin soon, with substantial deference to the interests and guidance of the 10 Western Pacific nations. Given the growing interests of Canada and Mexico in Pacific Ocean trade and other exchanges, perhaps they can even contribute their resources in some way to the effort. The potential of such a network is vast.

The Pacific Ocean grows smaller as interdependencies grow stronger. Without question, continued collective prosperity rests largely on cooperative measures for protecting security and stability.

CSIS Pacific Basin Project

Purpose

The CSIS Pacific Basin Project is a scholarly research effort focusing on the nations of East Asia and the Pacific. It seeks to place the strategic and economic significance of the Asian-Pacific nations in global perspective, with special reference to the emerging identity of the regional Pacific Basin Community concept. Major attention is given to U.S. relationships with China, Taiwan, Korea, and Japan; with the ASEAN nations (Singapore, Malaysia, Indonesia, Thailand, and the Philippines); with Australia and New Zealand; and with the comprehensive Pacific region or "basin" as an increasingly interactive, interdependent community of nations. Thus, secondary attention is given to the related roles of the Soviet Union, Canada, and Latin America as they affect the future of Pacific-wide cooperation.

The Project, begun in 1978, is multidisciplinary in approach, concentrating on the interplay among political, economic, and security factors affecting the Asian-Pacific region and on the interconnection of that region with the United States. The objective is to promote mutual understanding and to provide objective information as well as analytical perspective for policy discussions in Washington about the individual nations of Asia and the Pacific Basin and about multilateral movements toward regional cooperation.

Accordingly, one important aspect of this program is to provide members of the U.S. Congress, their senior congressional staff advisers, and interested representatives of the academic and commercial sectors with timely information on these topics, along with the opportunity to discuss among themselves those political, economic, and security issues affecting the Pacific region and U.S. interests therein. This aspect of the project has been institutionalized through the creation in 1981 of a regular series of Congressional Study Group discussion seminars held at eight-week intervals on Capitol Hill.

Background

The Pacific Community—An Emerging Concept

The Asian-Pacific area has become one of the most dynamic regions in the world, comprising as it does some of the highest annual rates of national economic growth combined with an increasingly important strategic position for the region in world events. The phenomenal industrial development of Japan, South Korea, and Taiwan in recent years, together with the birth of ASEAN and its rapid economic progress, has created regional economic strength that compares favorably with that of the United States, the Soviet Union, or Western Europe.

Already the interdependencies among the economies of the various Pacific nations are nearly as complex and sophisticated as those of the European Common Market, a result of multinational commercial investments in the area, of expanding bilateral trade and trade competition, and of increasing routine contacts between regional corporations, businessmen, and economists in the individual countries. This new phenomenon of intensive regional economic interaction has created broad interest in establishing a tangible Pacific economic community framework, through which a variety of issues with regional causes and/or implications could be tackled systematically with regional approaches.

Because the United States remains directly and substantially involved in both the economic development and maintenance of stability in the Asian-Pacific region and because this nation is likely to be vitally involved as a participant in any such emerging Pacific Community framework, it is essential that American scholars, policymakers, and business representatives begin now to focus on the design and operation of various organizational models already under discussion in the Far East. In particular, Congress should begin to study the potential nature of U.S. involvement and the possible benefits of such an association. CSIS is especially well suited to assist by undertaking a scholarly program of congressional-oriented activities that will educate members and key staff personnel about the models and concepts under consideration, as well as to assist in the formulation of specific ideas about U.S. participation based on discussions with a cross-section of U.S. citizens interested in the area.

General Questions

Basic topics for inquiry within the Project framework include, but are not limited to, the following:

1. Proposals and prospects for establishing a Pacific Basin Economic Community and for expanding U.S. participation in regional economic development;
2. Enhancement of regional cooperation in trade and investment matters;
3. Energy production, use, exploration, conservation, and trade within the region (including both petroleum and nuclear resources);
4. Unique political and economic environments and regional roles of individual nations in the Pacific Basin area;

5. Potentially destabilizing political and social problems afflicting progress, including regional refugee flows, terrorist activities, etc;
6. The practical extent of interaction with the economic systems of China, the Soviet Union, and Vietnam;
7. Prospects for enhancing security and stability on the Korean Peninsula, across the Taiwan Strait, and in Southeast Asia;
8. Methods for defending and preserving free access to vital sea-lanes of communication against threats or obstructions of any kind.

Methods

The dynamic portion of the Project involves an interlocking series of seminars, conferences, study groups, and informal discussions among open-minded scholars, officials, and experts of all kinds of political, economic, and strategic matters who are able and willing to examine all options.

As part of this format, the CSIS will continue to host a series of luncheon seminars for key members of the U.S. Congress, other policymakers, academicians, and members of the private sector at which informal presentations and discussions on timely topics will take place; provide a forum for scholarly exchange of ideas with occasional overseas visitors to Washington; conduct continuing research on specific political and strategic issues affecting the regional economic environment; and publish research findings for general public distribution. The CSIS monthly newsletter, *Asia Report,* will continue to carry summary reports and analyses of current major economic, political, and strategic developments in the region. It is circulated regularly among Congressional offices, U.S. businesses, and academic institutions.

In addition, during 1983, the Pacific Basin Project organized a Pacific Community Correspondence Network with other regional academic institutions, for the purpose of exchanging new information on the Community cooperation topic. A major CSIS Conference on the findings of the Project is planned for October, 1983, with the participation of overseas delegations.

The CSIS Pacific Basin Congressional Study Group is under the direction of U.S. Senators Paul S. Trible (R-Va.), John Glenn (D-Ohio), and Frank Murkowski (R-Alaska), and Congressmen Stephen Solarz (D-N.Y.), and Joel Pritchard (R-Wash.). Membership includes a variety of U.S. executive branch officials, Asian-Pacific scholars, and corporate leaders who deal in regional commercial affairs. The discussion series will culminate in the October multinational CSIS Conference and the issuance of a final report late in 1983.

Related Activities

Special research and analysis is underway on political and strategic developments affecting the Korean Peninsula and the surrounding Northeast Asian area. This effort, under the direction of Dr. Seung Hwan Kim, combines intensive private research with an active program of public seminars and publications for maximum dissemination of the relevant data. In a similar manner, Dr. Dora Alves conducts research focusing particularly on Australia, the South Pacific, and Southeast Asia, as a complement to the broader Project concentration on the Asian-Pacific region as a whole.

Project Staff

Robert L. Downen, Director
Ray S. Cline, CSIS Senior Associate; Editor, *Asia Report*
Dora Alves, Research Associate for Southeast Asia and the South Pacific
Bruce J. Dickson, Research Consultant
Support Staff: Ann Campagna, JoAnn Walters, Theresa Williams

Publications

Northeast Asia: Prosperity and Vulnerability, Proceedings of a Workshop sponsored by Korea University and CSIS (1979) (*Significant Issues Series* Vol. I, No. 2)
The Taiwan Pawn in the China Game: Congress to the Rescue, by Robert L. Downen (1979) (*Significant Issues Series* Vol. I, No. 1)
Of Grave Concern: U.S.-Taiwan Relations on the Threshold of the 1980s, by Robert L. Downen (1981) (*Significant Issues Series* Vol. III, No. 4)
Multi-system Nations and International Law, edited by Hungdah Chiu and Robert L. Downen, with the University of Maryland (1981)
The Communist Five and the Capitalist Ten: Socio-Economic Systems in Asia, by Ray S. Cline and Marjorie W. Cline (1982) (Reprint from *The Journal of East Asia Affairs,* Vol. II, No. 1, Spring/Summer, 1982)
The Security of Taiwan: Unraveling the Dilemma, by Martin L. Lasater (1981) (*Significant Issues Series* Vol. IV, No. 1)

Northeast Asia in the 1980s: Challenge and Opportunity, Proceedings of a
  Conference (1983) Robert L. Downen, editor. (*Significant Issues Series*
  Vol. V, No. 2)
Asia Report, a CSIS monthly newsletter initiated in 1979

ᴸ

LIBRARY OF DAVIDSON COLLEGE

Books on regular loan may be checked out for **two weeks**. Books must be presented at the Circulation Desk in order to be renewed.

A fine is charged after date due.

Special books are subject to special regulations at the discretion of the library staff.